This book belongs to

....

....

THE PUFFIN
TWENTIETH-CENTURY
COLLECTION OF
VERSE

THE PUFFIN TWENTIETH-CENTURY COLLECTION OF VERSE

Edited by Brian Patten

PUFFIN BOOKS

VIKING/PUFFIN

Published by the Penguin Group
Penguin Books Ltd, 27 Wrights Lane, London W8 5TZ, England
Penguin Putnam Inc., 375 Hudson Street, New York, New York 10014, USA
Penguin Books Australia Ltd, Ringwood, Victoria, Australia
Penguin Books Canada Ltd, 10 Alcorn Avenue, Toronto, Ontario, Canada M4V 3B2
Penguin Books (NZ) Ltd, Private Bag 102902, NSMC, Auckland, New Zealand

On the World Wide Web at: www.penguin.com

Penguin Books Ltd, Registered Offices: Harmondsworth, Middlesex, England

First published 1999
1 3 5 7 9 10 8 6 4 2

This edition copyright © Penguin Books Ltd, 1999
All illustrations remain the copyright © of the individual illustrators credited, 1999
The acknowledgements on page 179 constitute an extension of this copyright page
All rights reserved

The moral right of the illustrators has been asserted

Set in 14pt Bembo

Manufactured in China by Imago Publishing Limited

British Library Cataloguing in Publication Data
A CIP catalogue record for this book is available from the British Library

ISBN 0–670–88522–3

Contents

BENJAMIN ZEPHANIAH   *Illustrated by Alison Chatterton*
Body Talk   *1*
This Orange Tree   *3*

GRACE NICHOLS   *Illustrated by Sheila Moxley*
Ar-a-rat   *4*

RICHARD EDWARDS   *Illustrated by Lydia Monks*
The Word Party   *5*
When I Was Three   *6*

JOHN AGARD   *Illustrated by Mary McQuillan*
Don't Call Alligator Long-Mouth Till You Cross River   *7*
Hatch Me a Riddle   *8*

MICHAEL DUGAN   *Illustrated by Anthony Lewis*
Nightening   *9*

MICHAEL ROSEN   *Illustrated by Korky Paul*
If You Don't Put Your Shoes On Before I Count Fifteen   *10*
I'm the Youngest in Our House   *12*

BRIAN PATTEN   *Illustrated by Alison Jay*
The Newcomer   *14*
Squeezes   *15*

KIT WRIGHT   *Illustrated by Emma Chichester Clark*
Laurie and Dorrie   *16*
Just Before Christmas   *17*

LIBBY HOUSTON   *Illustrated by Peter Bailey*
The Dream of the Cabbage Caterpillars   *19*
The Old Woman and the Sandwiches   *20*

JACK PRELUTSKY   *Illustrated by Lydia Monks*
Homework! Oh, Homework!   *21*
Today is Very Boring   *22*

DENNIS LEE   *Illustrated by Mary McQuillan*
Lizzy's Lion   24

ALLAN AHLBERG   *Illustrated by Fritz Wegner*
Billy McBone   27
I Did a Bad Thing Once   28

ROGER MCGOUGH   *Illustrated by Lydia Monks*
Three Rusty Nails   29
Sky in the Pie!   30

GARETH OWEN   *Illustrated by Anthony Lewis*
Dear Mr Examiner   32

NANCY WILLARD   *Illustrated by Rosamund Fowler*
Blake Leads a Walk on the Milky Way   34

ADRIAN MITCHELL   *Illustrated by Lydia Monks*
Stufferation   36

ADRIAN HENRI   *Illustrated by Peter Bailey*
Best Friends   39

SHEL SILVERSTEIN
Sick   40

TED HUGHES   *Illustrated by Chris Riddell*
Leaves   42

MARY ANN HOBERMAN   *Illustrated by Michael Terry*
Combinations   44

ELIZABETH JENNINGS   *Illustrated by Diz Wallis*
Lullaby   46

JAMES BERRY   *Illustrated by Sheila Moxley*
Dreaming Black Boy   47

VERNON SCANNELL   *Illustrated by Sue Williams*
Growing Pain   49

PHILIP LARKIN   *Illustrated by Peter Bailey*
Take One Home for the Kiddies   51

N. M. BODECKER
Perfect Arthur   52

RICHARD WILBUR   *Illustrated by Ruth Rivers*
Some Opposites   53

EDWIN MORGAN | Illustrated by Lydia Monks
The Computer's First Christmas Card | 54

MAX FATCHEN | Illustrated by Michael Terry
extract from Ruinous Rhymes | 56

JOHN HEATH-STUBBS | Illustrated by Sue Williams
The Kingfisher | 57

SPIKE MILLIGAN | Illustrated by the author
Lady B's Fleas | 58
The Ying-tong-iddle-I-po | 58

CHARLES CAUSLEY | Illustrated by Alison Jay
Tom Bone | 60
Colonel Fazackerley | 61

ROALD DAHL | Illustrated by Quentin Blake
Extract from The Witches | 63

EVE MERRIAM | Illustrated by Mary McQuillan
Catch a Little Rhyme | 66

JUDITH WRIGHT | Illustrated by Sue Williams
Magpies | 68

DYLAN THOMAS | Illustrated by Chris Riddell
The Song of The Mischievous Dog | 69

LAURIE LEE | Illustrated by Ruth Rivers
Apples | 70

GEORGE BARKER | Illustrated by Louisa St Pierre
They Call To One Another | 71

EDWARD LOWBURY | Illustrated by Bee Willey
The Huntsman | 73

IAN SERRAILLIER | Illustrated by Tim Clarey
The Visitor | 75

MERVYN PEAKE | Illustrated by Chris Riddell
Aunts and Uncles | 77

JOHN WALSH | Illustrated by Emma Chichester Clark
The Bully Asleep | 80

NORMAN MacCAIG | Illustrated by Ruth Rivers
Blind Horse | 82

MARGARET WISE BROWN   *Illustrated by Rosamund Fowler*
The Secret Song   84

JAMES REEVES   *Illustrated by Diz Wallis*
Spells   86
Rabbit and Lark   87

THEODORE ROETHKE   *Illustrated by Sue Williams*
My Papa's Waltz   89

KATHLEEN RAINE   *Illustrated by Sheila Moxley*
Spell of Creation   90

W. H. AUDEN   *Illustrated by Peter Bailey*
Night Mail   92

LYDIA PENDER   *Illustrated by Mary McQuillan*
Giants   95

SIR JOHN BETJEMAN   *Illustrated by Tim Clarey*
Diary of a Church Mouse   97

LEONARD CLARK   *Illustrated by Mary McQuillan*
Good Company   100

A. L. ROWSE   *Illustrated by Tom Saeker*
The White Cat of Trenarren   101

STEVIE SMITH   *Illustrated by Rosamund Fowler*
The Old Sweet Dove of Wiveton   104

OGDEN NASH   *Illustrated by Michael Terry*
The Wombat   106
The Purist   107

ROBERT GRAVES   *Illustrated by Bee Willey*
The Alice Jean   108
The Penny Fiddle   110

RACHEL FIELD   *Illustrated by Louisa St Pierre*
Something Told the Wild Geese   111

E. E. CUMMINGS   *Illustrated by Rosamund Fowler*
maggie and milly and molly and may   112

ELIZABETH COATSWORTH   *Illustrated by Ruth Rivers*
Song of the Rabbits Outside the Tavern   113

WILFRED OWEN   *Illustrated by Bee Willey*
Extract from The Little Mermaid   115

W. J. TURNER   *Illustrated by Bee Willey*
India   116

T. S. ELIOT
Skimbleshanks: The Railway Cat   117

RUPERT BROOKE   *Illustrated by Tom Saeker*
These I Have Loved   120

E. V. RIEU   *Illustrated by Lydia Monks*
Sir Smashum Uppe
                                                122

A. A. MILNE   *Illustrated by E. H. Shepard*
Lines and Squares   124
Daffodowndilly   125

ELEANOR FARJEON   *Illustrated by Emma Chichester Clark*
The Distance   126
The Sounds in the Evening   127

VACHEL LINDSAY   *Illustrated by Ruth Rivers*
The Flower-Fed Buffaloes   129

JOHN MASEFIELD   *Illustrated by Sue Williams*
An Old Song Re-Sung   130

EDWARD THOMAS   *Illustrated by Louisa St Pierre*
Snow   131

ROBERT SERVICE   *Illustrated by Justin Todd*
The Cremation of Sam McGee   132

HARRY GRAHAM   *Illustrated by Anthony Lewis*
Politeness   138

ROBERT FROST   *Illustrated by Sheila Moxley*
Stopping by Woods on a Snowy Evening   139
A Minor Bird   140

G. K. CHESTERTON   *Illustrated by Bee Willey*
The Donkey   141

WALTER DE LA MARE   *Illustrated by Rosamund Fowler*
Tom's Angel 142
The Scarecrow 143
A Robin 144

W. H. DAVIES   *Illustrated by Tim Clarey*
The Blind Boxer 145
The Happy Child 147

HILAIRE BELLOC   *Illustrated by Michael Terry*
The Vulture 148
The Frog 149

MARY GILMORE   *Illustrated by Tom Saeker*
The Wild Horses 150

W. B. YEATS   *Illustrated by Ruth Rivers*
The Song of Wandering Aengus 152

RUDYARD KIPLING
A Smuggler's Song 154

A. B. (BANJO) PATERSON   *Illustrated by Sheila Moxley*
Waltzing Matilda 156

A. E. HOUSMAN   *Illustrated by Diz Wallis*
When Green Buds Hang 158

KATHARINE PYLE   *Illustrated by Anthony Lewis*
The Toys Talk of the World 159

THOMAS HARDY   *Illustrated by Ruth Rivers*
Snow in the Suburbs 161
Transformations 163

INDEX OF POETS 164

INDEX OF FIRST LINES 166

BIOGRAPHICAL NOTES 169

ACKNOWLEDGEMENTS 179

BENJAMIN ZEPHANIAH

Body Talk

Dere's a Sonnet
Under me bonnet
Dere's a Epic
In me ear,
Dere's a Novel
In me navel
Dere's a Classic
Here somewhere.
Dere's a Movie
In me left knee
A long story
In me right,
Dere's a shorty
Inbetweeny
It is tickly
In de night.
Dere's a picture
In me ticker
Unmixed riddims
In me heart,
In me texture
Dere's a comma

In me fat chin
Dere is Art.
Dere's an Opera
In me bladder
A Ballad's
In me wrist
Dere is laughter
In me shoulder
In me guzzard's
A nice twist.
In me dreadlocks
Dere is syntax
A dance kicks
In me bum
Thru me blood tracks
Dere run true facts
I got limericks
From me Mum,
Documentaries
In me entries
Plays on history
In me folk,
Dere's a Trilogy
When I tink of three
On me toey
Dere's a joke.

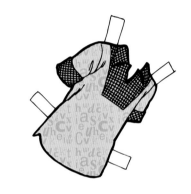

This Orange Tree

I touched my first rose
Under this orange tree,
I was young and fruity
The sweet rose was blooming.

I found faith
Under this orange tree
It was here all the time.
One day I picked it up
Then I realized
How great you are.

It was under this
Very orange tree
That I read
My first Martin Luther King speech.
How great the word.

It was here
Under this very orange tree,
On this very peace of earth
That I first sang
With a hummingbird.
How great the song.

This orange tree knows me,
It is my friend,
I trust it and
It taste good.

GRACE NICHOLS

Ar-a-rat

I know a rat on Ararat,
He isn't thin, he isn't fat
Never been chased by any cat
Not that rat on Ararat.
He's sitting high on a mountain breeze,
Never tasted any cheese,
Never chewed up any old hat,
Not that rat on Ararat.
He just sits alone on a mountain breeze,
Wonders why the trees are green,
Ponders why the ground is flat,
O that rat on Ararat.
His eyes like saucers, glow in the dark –
The last to slip from Noah's ark.

RICHARD EDWARDS

The Word Party

Loving words clutch crimson roses,
Rude words sniff and pick their noses,
Sly words come dressed up as foxes,
Short words stand on cardboard boxes,
Common words tell jokes and gabble,
Complicated words play Scrabble,
Swear words stamp around and shout,
Hard words stare each other out,
Foreign words look lost and shrug,
Careless words trip on the rug,
Long words slouch with stooping shoulders,
Code words carry secret folders,
Silly words flick rubber bands,
Hyphenated words hold hands,
Strong words show off, bending metal,
Sweet words call each other 'petal',
Small words yawn and suck their thumbs
Till at last the morning comes.
Kind words give out farewell posies . . .

Snap! The dictionary closes.

5

When I Was Three

When I was three I had a friend
Who asked me why bananas bend,
I told him why, but now I'm four
I'm not so sure . . .

JOHN AGARD

Don't Call Alligator Long-Mouth Till You Cross River

Call alligator long-mouth
call alligator saw-mouth
call alligator pushy-mouth
call alligator scissors-mouth
call alligator raggedy-mouth
call alligator bumpy-bum
call alligator all dem rude word
but better wait
          till you cross river.

Hatch Me a Riddle

In a little white room
all round and smooth
sits a yellow moon.

In a little white room
once open, for ever open,
sits a yellow moon.

In a little white room,
with neither window nor door,
sits a yellow moon.

Who will break the walls
of the little white room
to steal the yellow moon?

A wise one or a fool?

MICHAEL DUGAN

Nightening

When you wake up at night
And it's dark and frightening,
Climb out of bed
And turn on the lightening.

MICHAEL ROSEN

If You Don't Put Your Shoes On Before I Count Fifteen

If you don't put your shoes on before I count fifteen
then we won't go to the woods to climb the chestnut
  one
        But I can't find them
Two
        I can't
They're under the sofa three
          No
          O yes
Four five six
        Stop – they've got knots they've got knots
You should untie the laces when you take your shoes
  off seven
        Will you do one shoe while I do the other
          then?
Eight but that would be cheating
        Please
All right
        It always . . .
Nine

It always sticks – I'll use my teeth

Ten

It won't it won't

It has – look.

Eleven

I'm not wearing any socks

Twelve

Stop counting stop counting. Mum where
are my socks mum

They're in your shoes. Where you left them.

I didn't

Thirteen

O they're inside out and upside down and
bundled up

Fourteen

Have you done the knot on the shoe you
were . . .

Yes

Put it on the right foot

But socks don't have right and wrong foot

The shoes silly

Fourteen and a half

I am I am. Wait.

Don't go to the woods without me

Look that's one shoe already

Fourteen and threequarters

There

You haven't tied the bows yet

We could do them on the way there

$14\frac{7}{8}...$ $14\frac{15}{16}...$

No we won't fourteen and seven eighths
      Help me then
      You know I'm not fast at bows
Fourteen and fifteen sixteeeeenths
      A single bow is all right isn't it
Fifteen we're off
      See I did it.
      Didn't I?

I'm the Youngest in Our House

I'm the youngest in our house
so it goes like this:

My brother comes in and says:
'Tell him to clear the fluff
out from under his bed.'
Mum says,
'Clear the fluff
out from under your bed.'
Father says,
'You heard what your mother said.'
'What?' I say.

'The fluff,' he says.
'Clear the fluff
out from under your bed.'
So I say,
'There's fluff under his bed, too,
you know.'
So Father says,
'But we're talking about the fluff
under *your* bed.'
'You will clear it up
won't you?' Mum says.
So now my brother – all puffed up –
says,
'Clear the fluff
out from under your bed,
clear the fluff
out from under your bed.'

Now I'm angry. I am angry.
So I say – what shall I say?
I say,
'Shuttup Stinks
YOU CAN'T RULE MY LIFE.'

BRIAN PATTEN

The Newcomer

'There's something new in the river,'
The fish said as it swam,
'It's got no scales, no fins, no gills,
And ignores the impassable dam.'

'There's something new in the trees,'
I heard a bloated thrush sing,
'It's got no beak, no claws, no feathers,
And not even the ghost of a wing.'

'There's something new in the warren,'
The rabbit said to the doe,
'It's got no fur, no eyes, no paws,
Yet digs deeper than we can go.'

'There's something new in the whiteness,'
Said the snow-bright polar-bear,
'I saw its shadow on a glacier
But it left no foot-prints there.'

Throughout the animal kingdom
The news was spreading fast –

No beak no claws no feathers,
No scales no fur no gills,
It lives in the trees and the water,
In the earth and the snow and the hills,
And it kills and it kills and it kills.

Squeezes

We love to squeeze bananas,
We love to squeeze ripe plums,
And when they are feeling sad
We love to squeeze our mums.

KIT WRIGHT

Laurie and Dorrie

The first thing that you'll notice if
   You meet my Uncle Laurie
Is how, whatever else he does,
   He can't stop saying sorry.

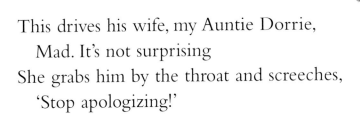

He springs from bed at 5 a.m.
   As birds begin to waken,
Cries, 'No offence intended, lads –
   Likewise, I hope, none taken!'

This drives his wife, my Auntie Dorrie,
   Mad. It's not surprising
She grabs him by the throat and screeches,
   'Stop apologizing!'

My Uncle, who's a little deaf,
   Says, 'Sorry? Sorry, Dorrie?'
'For goodness' sake,' Aunt Dorrie screams,
   'Stop saying sorry, Laurie!'

'Sorry, dear? Stop saying what?'
  'SORRY!' Laurie's shaken.
'No need to be, my dear,' he says,
  'For *no offence is taken*.

Likewise I'm sure that there was none
  Intended on your part.'
'Dear Lord,' Aunt Dorrie breathes, 'what can
  I do, where do I start?'

Then, 'Oh, I *see*,' says Uncle L.,
  'You mean "stop saying sorry"!
I'm sorry to have caused offence –
  Oops! Er . . . *sorry*, Dorrie!'

Just Before Christmas

Down the Holloway Road on the top of the bus
On the just-before-Christmas nights we go,
Allie and me and all of us,
And we look at the lit-up shops below.
Orange and yellow the fruit stalls glow,
Store windows are sploshed with sort-of-snow,
And Santa's a poor old so-and-so,
With his sweating gear and his sack in tow,
And Christ . . . mas is coming!

At the front of the top of the lit-up bus
Way down the Holloway Road we ride,
Allie and me and all of us,
And the butchers chop and lop with pride,
And the turkeys squat with their stuffing inside
By ropes of sausages soon to be fried,
And every door is open wide
As down the road we growl or glide
And Christ . . . mas is coming!

All at the front of the top of the bus,
Far down the Holloway Road we roar,
Allie and me and all of us,
And tellies are tinselled in every store,
With fairy lights over every door,
With glitter and crêpe inside, what's more,
And everyone seeming to say, 'For sure,
Christmas is coming as never before.'
Yes, Christ . . . mas is coming!

LIBBY HOUSTON

The Dream of the Cabbage Caterpillars

There was no magic spell:
   all of us, sleeping,
dreamt the same dream – a dream
   that's ours for the keeping.

In sunbeam or dripping rain,
   sister by brother
we once roamed with glee
   the leaves that our mother

laid us and left us on,
   browsing our fill
of green cabbage, fresh cabbage,
   thick cabbage, until

in the hammocks we hung
   from the garden wall
came sleep, and the dream
   that changed us all –

we had left our soft bodies,
　　the munching, the crawling,
to skim through the clear air
　　like white petals falling!

Just so, so we woke –
　　so to skip high as towers,
and dip now to sweet fuel
　　from trembling bright flowers.

The Old Woman and the Sandwiches

I met a wizened wood-woman
　　Who begged a crumb of me.
Four sandwiches of ham I had:
　　I gave her three.

'Bless you, thank you, kindly Miss,
　　Shall be rewarded well –
Three everlasting gifts, whose value
　　None can tell.'

'Three wishes?' out I cried in glee –
　　'No, gifts you may not choose:
A flea and gnat to bite your back
　　And gravel in your shoes.'

JACK PRELUTSKY

Homework! Oh, Homework!

Homework! Oh, homework!
I hate you! You stink!
I wish I could wash you
away in the sink,
if only a bomb
would explode you to bits.
Homework! Oh, homework!
You're giving me fits.

I'd rather take baths
with a man-eating shark,
or wrestle a lion
alone in the dark,
eat spinach and liver,
pet ten porcupines,
than tackle the homework
my teacher assigns.

Homework! Oh, homework!
You're last on my list,
I simply can't see
why you even exist,
if you just disappeared
it would tickle me pink.
Homework! Oh, homework!
I hate you! You stink!

Today is Very Boring

Today is very boring,
it's a very boring day,
there is nothing much to look at,
there is nothing much to say,
there's a peacock on my sneakers,
there's a penguin on my head,
there's a dormouse on my doorstep,
I am going back to bed.

Today is very boring,
it is boring through and through,
there is absolutely nothing
that I think I want to do,
I see giants riding rhinos,
and an ogre with a sword,
there's a dragon blowing smoke rings,
I am positively bored.

22

Today is very boring,
I can hardly help but yawn,
there's a flying saucer landing
in the middle of my lawn,
a volcano just erupted
less than half a mile away,
and I think I felt an earthquake,
it's a very boring day.

23

DENNIS LEE

Lizzy's Lion

Lizzy had a lion
    With a big, bad roar,
And she kept him in the bedroom
    By the closet-cupboard door;

Lizzy's lion wasn't friendly
    Lizzy's lion wasn't tame –
Not unless you learned to call him
    By his Secret Lion Name.

One dark night, a rotten robber
    With a rotten robber mask
Snuck in through the bedroom window –
    And he didn't even ask.

And he brought a bag of candy
    That was sticky-icky-sweet,
Just to make friends with a lion
    (If a lion he should meet).

First he sprinkled candy forwards,
    Then he sprinkled candy back;
Then he picked up Lizzy's piggy-bank
    And stuck it in his sack.

But as the rotten robber
    Was preparing to depart,
Good old Lizzy's lion wakened
    With a snuffle and a start.

And he muttered, 'Candy? – piffle!'
    And he rumbled, 'Candy? – pooh!'
And he gave the rotten robber
    An experimental chew.

Then the robber shooed the lion,
    Using every name he knew;
But each time he shooed, the lion
    Merely took another chew.

It was: 'Down, Fido! Leave, Leo!
    Shoo, you good old boy!'
But the lion went on munching
    With a look of simple joy.

It was: 'Stop, Mopsy! Scram, Sambo!
    This is a disgrace!'
But the lion went on lunching
    With a smile upon his face.

Then old Lizzy heard the rumble,
    And old Lizzy heard the fight,
And old Lizzy got her slippers
    And turned on the bedroom light.

There was robber on the toy-shelf!
    There was robber on the rug!
There was robber in the lion
    (Who was looking rather smug)!

But old Lizzy wasn't angry,
    And old Lizzy wasn't rough.
She simply said the Secret Name:
    'Lion! – that's enough.'

Then old Lizzy and her Lion
    Took the toes & tum & head,
And they put them in the garbage,
    And they both went back to bed.

ALLAN AHLBERG

Billy McBone

Billy McBone
Had a mind of his own,
Which he mostly kept under his hat.
The teachers all thought
That he couldn't be taught,
But Bill didn't seem to mind that.

Billy McBone
Had a mind of his own,
Which the teachers had searched for for years.
Trying test after test,
They still never guessed
It was hidden between his ears.

Billy McBone
Had a mind of his own,
Which only his friends ever saw.
When the teacher said, 'Bill,
Whereabouts is Brazil?'
He just shuffled and stared at the floor.

Billy McBone
Had a mind of his own,
Which he kept under lock and key.
While the teachers in vain
Tried to burgle his brain,
Bill's thoughts were off wandering free.

I Did a Bad Thing Once

I did a bad thing once.
I took this money from my mother's purse
For bubble gum.
What made it worse,
She bought me some
For being good, while I'd been vice versa
So to speak – that made it worser.

ROGER McGOUGH

Three Rusty Nails

Mother, there's a strange man
Waiting at the door
With a familiar sort of face
You feel you've seen before.

Says his name is Jesus
Can we spare a couple of bob
Says he's been made redundant
And now can't find a job.

Yes I think he is a foreigner
Egyptian or a Jew
Oh aye, and that reminds me
He'd like some water too.

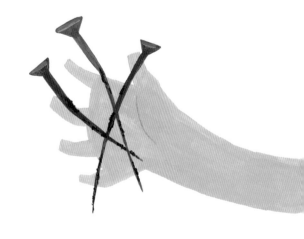

Well shall I give him what he wants
Or send him on his way?
OK I'll give him 5p
Say that's all we've got today.

And I'll forget about the water
I suppose it's a bit unfair
But honest, he's filthy dirty
All beard and straggly hair.

Mother, he asked about the water
I said the tank had burst
Anyway I gave him the money
That seemed to quench his thirst.

He said it was little things like that
That kept him on the rails
Then he gave me his autographed picture
And these three rusty nails.

Sky in the Pie!

Waiter, there's a sky in my pie
Remove it at once if you please
You can keep your incredible sunsets
I ordered mincemeat and cheese

I can't stand nightingales singing
Or clouds all burnished with gold
The whispering breeze is disturbing the peas
And making my chips go all cold

I don't care if the chef is an artist
Whose canvases hang in the Tate
I want two veg. and puff pastry
Not the Universe heaped on my plate

OK I'll try just a spoonful
I suppose I've got nothing to lose
Mm . . . the colours quite tickle the palette
With a blend of delicate hues

The sun has a custardy flavour
And the clouds are as light as air
And the wind a chewier texture
(With a hint of cinnamon there?)

This sky is simply delicious
Why haven't I tried it before?
I can chew my way through to Eternity
And still have room left for more

Having acquired a taste for the Cosmos
I'll polish this sunset off soon
I can't wait to tuck into the night sky
Waiter! Please bring me the Moon!

GARETH OWEN

Dear Mr Examiner

Thank you so much for your questions
I've read them most carefully through
But there isn't a single one of them
That I know the answer to.

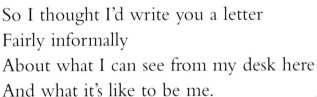

I've written my name as instructed
Put the year, the month and the day
But after I'd finished doing that
I had nothing further to say.

So I thought I'd write you a letter
Fairly informally
About what I can see from my desk here
And what it's like to be me.

Mandy has written ten pages
But it's probably frightful guff
And Angela Smythe is copying
The answers off her cuff.

Miss Quinlan is marking our homework
The clock keeps ticking away
I suppose for anyone outside
It's just another day.

There'll be mothers going on errands
Grandmothers sipping tea
Unemployed men doing crosswords
or watching 'Crown Court' on TV.

The rain has finally stopped here
The sun has started to shine
And in a back garden in Sefton Drive
A housewife hangs shirts on a line.

A class files past to play tennis
The cathedral clock has just pealed
A mower chugs backwards and forwards
Up on the hockey field.

Miss Quinlan's just read what I've written
Her face is an absolute mask
Before she collects the papers in
I've a sort of favour to ask.

I thought your questions were lovely
I've only myself to blame
But couldn't you give me some marks
For writing the date and my name.

NANCY WILLARD

Blake Leads a Walk on the Milky Way

He gave silver shoes to the rabbit
and golden gloves to the cat
and emerald boots to the tiger and me
and boots of iron to the rat.

He inquired, 'Is everyone ready?
The night is uncommonly cold.
We'll start on our journey as children,
but I fear we will finish it old.'

He hurried us to the horizon
where morning and evening meet.
The slippery stars went skipping
under our hapless feet.

'I'm terribly cold,' said the rabbit.
'My paws are becoming quite blue,
and what will become of my right thumb
while you admire the view?'

'The stars,' said the cat, 'are abundant
and falling on every side.
Let them carry us back to our comforts.
Let us take the stars for a ride.'

'I shall garland my room,' said the tiger,
'with a few of these emerald lights.'
'I shall give up sleeping forever,' I said.
'I shall never part day from night.'

The rat was sullen. He grumbled
he ought to have stayed in his bed.
'What's gathered by fools in heaven
will never endure,' he said.

Blake gave silver stars to the rabbit
and golden stars to the cat
and emerald stars to the tiger and me
but a handful of dirt to the rat.

ADRIAN MITCHELL

Stufferation

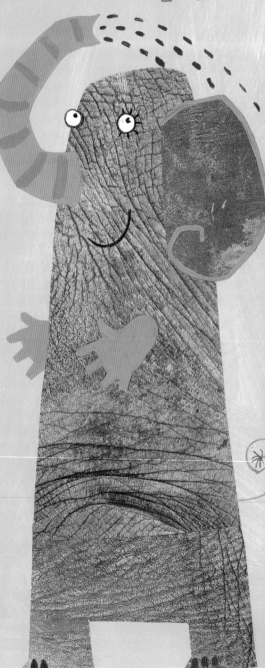

Lovers lie around in it
Broken glass is found in it
Grass
I like that stuff

Tuna fish get trapped in it
Legs come wrapped in it
Nylon
I like that stuff

Eskimos and tramps chew it
Madame Tussaud gave status to it
Wax
I like that stuff

Elephants get sprayed with it
Scotch is made with it
Water
I like that stuff

Clergy are dumbfounded by it
Bones are surrounded by it
Flesh
I like that stuff

Harps are strung with it
Mattresses are sprung with it
Wire
I like that stuff

Carpenters make cots of it
Undertakers use lots of it
Wood
I like that stuff

Cigarettes are lit by it
Pensioners get happy when they sit by it
Fire
I like that stuff

Dankworth's alto is made of it, most of it,
Scoobdidoo is composed of it
Plastic
I like that stuff

Apemen take it to make them hairier
I ate a ton of it in Bulgaria
Yoghurt
I like that stuff

Man-made fibres and raw materials
Old rolled gold and breakfast cereals
Platinum linoleum
I like that stuff

Skin on my hands
Hair on my head
Toenails on my feet
And linen on the bed

Well I like that stuff
Yes I like that stuff
The earth
Is made of earth
And I like that stuff

ADRIAN HENRI

Best Friends

It's Susan I talk to not Tracey,
Before that I sat next to Jane;
I used to be best friends with Lynda
But these days I think she's a pain.

Natasha's all right in small doses,
I meet Mandy sometimes in town;
I'm jealous of Annabel's pony
And I don't like Nicola's frown.

I used to go skating with Catherine,
Before that I went there with Ruth;
And Kate's so much better at trampoline:
She's a showoff, to tell you the truth.

I think that I'm going off Susan,
She borrowed my comb yesterday;
I *think* I might sit next to Tracey,
She's my nearly best friend: she's OK.

SHEL SILVERSTEIN

Sick

'I cannot go to school today,'
Said little Peggy Ann McKay.
'I have the measles and the mumps,
A gash, a rash and purple bumps.
My mouth is wet, my throat is dry,
I'm going blind in my right eye.
My tonsils are as big as rocks,
I've counted sixteen chicken pox
And there's one more – that's seventeen,
And don't you think my face looks green?
My leg is cut, my eyes are blue –
It might be instamatic flue.
I cough and sneeze and gasp and choke,
I'm sure that my left leg is broke –
My hip hurts when I move my chin,
My belly button's caving in,
My back is wrenched, my ankle's sprained,
My 'pendix pains each time it rains.
My nose is cold, my toes are numb,
I have a sliver in my thumb.
My neck is stiff, my spine is weak,
I hardly whisper when I speak.
My tongue is filling up my mouth,
I think my hair is falling out.

My elbow's bent, my spine ain't straight,
My temperature is one-o-eight.
My brain is shrunk, I cannot hear,
There is a hole inside my ear.
I have a hangnail, and my heart is – what?
What's that? What's that you say?
You say today is . . . Saturday?
G'bye, I'm going out to play!'

TED HUGHES

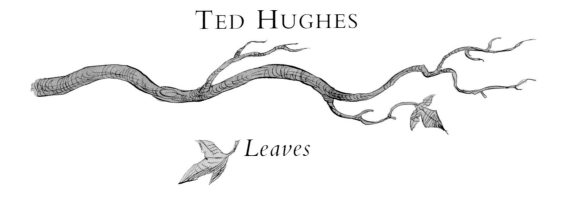

Leaves

Who's killed the leaves?
Me, says the apple, I've killed them all.
Fat as a bomb or a cannonball
I've killed the leaves.

Who sees them drop?
Me, says the pear, they will leave me all bare
So all the people can point and stare.
I see them drop.

Who'll catch their blood?
Me, me, me, says the marrow, the marrow.
I'll get so rotund that they'll need a wheelbarrow.
I'll catch their blood.

Who'll make their shroud?
Me, says the swallow, there's just time enough
Before I must pack all my spools and be off.
I'll make their shroud.

Who'll dig their grave?
Me, says the river, with the power of the clouds
A brown deep grave I'll dig under my floods.
I'll dig their grave.

Who'll be their parson?
Me, says the Crow, for it is well-known
I study the bible right down to the bone.
I'll be their parson.

Who'll be chief mourner?
Me, says the wind, I will cry through the grass
The people will pale and go cold when I pass.
I'll be chief mourner.

Who'll carry the coffin?
Me, says the sunset, the whole world will weep
To see me lower it into the deep.
I'll carry the coffin.

Who'll sing a psalm?
Me, says the tractor, with my gear grinding glottle
I'll plough up the stubble and sing through my throttle.
I'll sing the psalm.

Who'll toll the bell?
Me, says the robin, my song in October
Will tell the still gardens the leaves are over.
I'll toll the bell.

MARY ANN HOBERMAN

Combinations

A flea flew by a bee. The bee
To flee the flea flew by a fly.
The fly flew high to flee the bee
Who flew to flee the flea who flew
To flee the fly who now flew by.

The bee flew by the fly. The fly
To flee the bee flew by the flea.
The flea flew high to flee the fly
Who flew to flee the bee who flew
To flee the flea who now flew by.

The fly flew by the flea. The flea
To flee the fly flew by the bee.
The bee flew high to flee the flea
Who flew to flee the fly who flew
To flee the bee who now flew by.

The flea flew by the fly. The fly
To flee the flea flew by the bee.
The bee flew high to flee the fly
Who flew to flee the flea who flew
To flee the bee who now flew by.

The fly flew by the bee. The bee
To flee the fly flew by the flea.
The flea flew high to flee the bee
Who flew to flee the fly who flew
To flee the flea who now flew by.

The bee flew by the flea. The flea
To flee the bee flew by the fly.
The fly flew high to flee the flea
Who flew to flee the bee who flew
To flee the fly who now flew by.

ELIZABETH JENNINGS

Lullaby

Sleep, my baby, the night is coming soon.
Sleep, my baby, the day has broken down.

Sleep now: let silence come, let the shadows form
A castle of strength for you, a fortress of calm.

You are so small, sleep will come with ease.
Hush now, be still now, join the silences.

JAMES BERRY

Dreaming Black Boy

I wish my teacher's eyes wouldn't
go past me today. Wish he'd know
it's okay to hug me when I kick
a goal. Wish I myself wouldn't
hold back when an answer comes.
I'm no woodchopper now
like all ancestors.

I wish I could be educated
to the best of tune up, and earn
good money and not sink to lick
boots. I wish I could go on every
crisscross way of the globe
and no persons or powers or
hotel keepers would make it a waste.

I wish life wouldn't spend me out
opposing. Wish same way creation
would have me stand it would have
me stretch, and hold high, my voice
Paul Robeson's, my inside eye
a sun. Nobody wants to say
hello to nasty answers.

I wish torch throwers of night
would burn lights for decent times.
Wish plotters in pyjamas would pray
for themselves. Wish people wouldn't
talk as if I dropped from Mars.

I wish only boys were scared
behind bravados, for I could suffer
I could suffer a big big lot.
I wish nobody would want to earn
the terrible burden I can suffer.

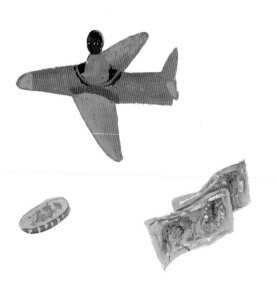

VERNON SCANNELL

Growing Pain

The boy was barely five years old.
We sent him to the little school
And left him there to learn the names
Of flowers in jam jars on the sill
And learn to do as he was told.
He seemed quite happy there until
Three weeks afterwards, at night,
The darkness whimpered in his room.
I went upstairs, switched on his light,
And found him wide awake, distraught,
Sheets mangled and his eiderdown
Untidy carpet on the floor.
I said, 'Why can't you sleep? A pain?'
He snuffled, gave a little moan,

And then he spoke a single word:
'Jessica.' The sound was blurred.
'Jessica? What do you mean?'
'A girl at school called Jessica,
She hurts –' he touched himself between
The heart and stomach '– she has been
Aching here and I can see her.'
Nothing I had read or heard
Instructed me in what to do.
I covered him and stroked his head.
'The pain will go, in time,' I said.

PHILIP LARKIN

Take One Home for the Kiddies

On shallow straw, in shadeless glass,
Huddled by empty bowls, they sleep:
No dark, no dam, no earth, no grass –
Mam, get us one of them to keep.

Living toys are something novel,
But it soon wears off somehow.
Fetch the shoebox, fetch the shovel –
Mam, we're playing funerals now.

N. M. BODECKER

Perfect Arthur

'Nowhere in the world,'
said Arthur,
'nowhere in the world,'
said he,
'is a boy
as absolutely
*per*fectly
perfect
as me!'

'Or, on second thought,'
said Arthur,
as he caught his mother's eye,
'should I say,
as absolutely
*per*fectly
perfect
as I?'

RICHARD WILBUR

Some Opposites

What is the opposite of *riot*?
It's *lots of people keeping quiet.*

The opposite of *doughnut*? Wait
A minute while I meditate.
This isn't easy. Ah, I've found it!
A cookie with a hole around it.

What is the opposite of *two*?
A lonely me, a lonely you.

The opposite of a *cloud* could be
A white reflection in the sea,
Or *a huge blueness in the air,*
Caused by a cloud's not being there.

The opposite of *opposite*?
That's much too difficult. I quit.

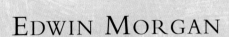

EDWIN MORGAN

The Computer's First Christmas Card

jollymerry
hollyberry
jollyberry
merryholly
happyjolly
jollyjelly
jellybelly
bellymerry
hollyheppy
jollyMolly
marryJerry
merryHarry
happyBarry
heppyJarry
boppyheppy
berryjorry
jorryjolly
moppyjelly
Mollymerry
Jerryjolly
bellyboppy
jorryhoppy

hollymoppy
Barrymerry
Jarryhappy
happyboppy
boppyjolly
jollymerry
merrymerry
merrymerry
merryChris
ammerryasa
Chrismerry
asMERRYCHR
YSANTHEMUM

MAX FATCHEN

Extract from Ruinous Rhymes

Pussycat, pussycat, where have you been,
Licking your lips with your whiskers so clean?
Pussycat, pussycat, purring and pudgy,
Pussycat, pussycat. WHERE IS OUR BUDGIE?

JOHN HEATH-STUBBS

The Kingfisher

When Noah left the Ark, the animals
Capered and gambolled on the squadgy soil,
Enjoying their new-found freedom; and the birds
Soared upwards, twittering, to the open skies.

But one soared higher than the rest, in utter ecstasy,
Till all his back and wings were drenched
With the vivid blue of heaven itself, and his breast scorched
With the upward-slanting rays of the setting sun.
When he came back to earth, he had lost the Ark;
His friends were all dispersed. So now he soars no more;
A lonely bird, he darts and dives for fish,
By streams and pools – places where water is –
Still searching, but in vain, for the vanished Ark
And rain-washed terraces of Ararat.

SPIKE MILLIGAN

Lady B's Fleas

Lady Barnaby takes her ease
    Knitting overcoats for fleas
By this kindness, fleas are smitten
    That's why she's *very rarely* bitten.

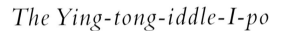

The Ying-tong-iddle-I-po

My Uncle Jim-jim
Had for years
Suffered from
Protruding ears.

Each morning then,
When he got up,
They stuck out like handles
on the F.A. Cup.

He tied them back
With bits of string
But they shot out again
With a noisy – *PING!*

They flapped in the wind
And in the rain,
Filled up with water
Then emptied again.

One morning Jim–jim
Fell out of bed
and got a Po
Stuck on his head.

He gave a Whoop,
A happy shout,
His ears no longer now
Stuck out.

For the rest of his days
He wore that Po,
But now at night
He has nowhere to go.

Tom Bone

My name is Tom Bone,
I live all alone
In a deep house on Winter Street.
    Through my mud wall
    The wolf-spiders crawl
    And the mole has his beat.

On my roof of green grass
All the day footsteps pass
In the heat and the cold,
    As snug in a bed
    With my name at its head
    One great secret I hold.

Tom Bone, when the owls rise
In the drifting night skies
Do you walk round about?
    All the solemn hours through
    I lie down just like you
    And sleep the night out.

Tom Bone, as you lie there
On your pillow of hair,
What grave thoughts do you keep?
   Tom says, 'Nonsense and stuff!
   You'll know soon enough.
   Sleep, darling, sleep.'

Colonel Fazackerley

Colonel Fazackerley Butterworth-Toast
Bought an old castle complete with a ghost,
But someone or other forgot to declare
To Colonel Fazack that the spectre was there.

On the very first evening, while waiting to dine,
The Colonel was taking a fine sherry wine,
When the ghost, with a furious flash and a flare,
Shot out of the chimney and shivered, 'Beware!'

Colonel Fazackerley put down his glass
And said, 'My dear fellow, that's really first class!
I just can't conceive how you do it at all.
I imagine you're going to a Fancy Dress Ball?'

At this, the dread ghost gave a withering cry.
Said the Colonel (his monocle firm in his eye),
'Now just how you do it I wish I could think.
Do sit down and tell me, and please have a drink.'

The ghost in his phosphorous cloak gave a roar
And floated about between ceiling and floor.
He walked through a wall and returned through a pane
And back up the chimney and came down again.

Said the Colonel, 'With laughter I'm feeling quite weak!'
(As trickles of merriment ran down his cheek).
'My house-warming party I hope you won't spurn.
You *must* say you'll come and you'll give us a turn!'

At this, the poor spectre – quite out of his wits –
Proceeded to shake himself almost to bits.
He rattled his chains and he clattered his bones
And he filled the whole castle with mumbles and moans.

But Colonel Fazackerley, just as before,
Was simply delighted and called out, 'Encore!'
At which the ghost vanished, his efforts in vain,
And never was seen at the castle again.

'Oh dear, what a pity!' said Colonel Fazack.
'I don't know his name, so I can't call him back.'
And then with a smile that was hard to define,
Colonel Fazackerley went in to dine.

Roald Dahl

Extract from The Witches

'Down vith children! Do them in!
Boil their bones and fry their skin!
Bish them, sqvish them, bash them, mash
   them!
Brrreak them, shake them, slash them, smash
   them!
Offer chocs vith magic powder!
Say "Eat up!" then say it louder.
Crrram them full of sticky eats,
Send them home still guzzling sveets.
And in the morning little fools
Go marching off to separate schools.
A girl feels sick and goes all pale.
She yells, "Hey look! I've grrrown a tail!"
A boy who's standing next to her
Screams, "Help! I think I'm grrrowing fur!"
Another shouts, "Vee look like frrreaks!
There's viskers growing on our cheeks!"
A boy who vos extremely tall
Cries out, "Vot's wrong? I'm grrrowing small!"

Four tiny legs begin to sprrrout
From everybody rrround about.
And all at vunce, all in a trrrice,
There are no children! Only MICE!

In every school is mice galore
All rrrunning rrround the school-rrroom floor!
And all the poor demented teachers
Is yelling, "Hey, who are these crrreatures?"
They stand upon the desks and shout,
"Get out, you filthy mice! Get out!
Vill someone fetch some mouse-trrraps,
    please!
And don't forrrget to bring the cheese!"
Now mousetrrraps come and every trrrap
Goes *snippy-snip* and *snappy-snap*.
The mouse-trrraps have a powerful spring,
The springs go *crack* and *snap* and *ping*!
Is lovely noise for us to hear!
Is music to a vitch's ear!
Dead mice is every place arrround,
Piled two feet deep upon the grrround,
Vith teachers searching left and rrright,
But not a single child in sight!
The teachers cry, "Vot's going on?
Oh vhere have all the children gone?
Is half-past nine and as a rrrule
They're never late as this for school!"
Poor teachers don't know vot to do.
Some sit and rrread, and just a few

Amuse themselves throughout the day
By sveeping all the mice avay.
AND ALL US VITCHES SHOUT HOORAY!'

EVE MERRIAM

Catch a Little Rhyme

Once upon a time
I caught a little rhyme

I set it on the floor
but it ran right out the door

I chased it on my bicycle
but it melted to an icicle

I scooped it up in my hat
but it turned into a cat

I caught it by the tail
but it stretched into a whale

I followed it in a boat
but it changed into a goat

When I fed it tin and paper
it became a tall skyscraper

Then it grew into a kite
and flew far out of sight . . .

JUDITH WRIGHT

Magpies

Along the road the magpies walk
with hands in pockets, left and right.
They tilt their heads, and stroll and talk.
In their well-fitted black and white

they look like certain gentlemen
who seem most nonchalant and wise
until their meal is served – and then
what clashing beaks, what greedy eyes!

But not one man that I have heard
throws back his head in such a song
of grace and praise – no man nor bird.
Their greed is brief; their joy is long.
For each is born with such a throat
as thanks his God with every note.

DYLAN THOMAS

The Song of the Mischievous Dog

There are many who say that a dog has its day,
    And a cat has a number of lives;
There are others who think that a lobster is pink,
    And that bees never work in their hives.
There are fewer, of course, who insist that a horse
    Has a horn and two humps on its head,
And a fellow who jests that a mare can build nests
    Is as rare as a donkey that's red.
Yet in spite of all this, I have moments of bliss,
    For I cherish a passion for bones,
And though doubtful of biscuit, I'm willing to risk it,
    And I love to chase rabbits and stones.
But my greatest delight is to take a good bite
    At a calf that is plump and delicious;
And if I indulge in a bite at a bulge,
    Let's hope you won't think me too vicious.

LAURIE LEE

Apples

Behold the apples' rounded worlds:
juice-green of July rain,
the black polestar of flower, the rind
mapped with its crimson stain.

The russet, crab and cottage red
burn to the sun's hot brass,
then drop like sweat from every branch
and bubble in the grass.

They lie as wanton as they fall,
and where they fall and break,
the stallion clamps his crunching jaws,
the starling stabs his beak.

In each plump gourd the cidery bite
of boys' teeth tears the skin;
the waltzing wasp consumes his share,
the bent worm enters in.

I, with as easy hunger, take
entire my season's dole;
welcome the ripe, the sweet, the sour,
the hollow and the whole.

GEORGE BARKER

They Call to One Another

They call to one another
    in the prisons of the sea
the mermen and mermaidens
    bound under lock and key
down in the green and salty dens
    and dungeons of the sea,
lying about in chains but
    dying to be free:
and this is why shortsighted men
    believe them not to be
for down to their dark dungeons it
    is very hard to see.

But sometimes morning fishermen
   drag up in the net
bits of bright glass or the silver comb
   of an old vanity set
or a letter rather hard to read
   because it is still wet
sent to remind us never, never
   never to forget
the mermen and mermaidens
   in the prisons of the sea
who call to one another
   when the stars of morning rise
and the stars of evening set
   for I have heard them calling
and I can hear them, yet.

EDWARD LOWBURY

The Huntsman

Kagwa hunted the lion,
   Through bush and forest went his spear.
One day he found the skull of a man
   And said to it, 'How did you come here?'
The skull opened its mouth and said,
   'Talking brought me here.'

   Kagwa hurried home;
      Went to the king's chair and spoke:
   'In the forest I found a talking skull.'
      The king was silent. Then he said slowly,
'Never since I was born of my mother
   Have I seen or heard of a skull which spoke.'

The king called out to his guards:
   'Two of you now go with him
And find this talking skull;
   But if his tale is a lie
And the skull speaks no word,
   This Kagwa himself must die.'

They rode into the forest;
   For days and nights they found nothing.
At last they saw the skull; Kagwa
   Said to it, 'How did you come here?'
The skull said nothing. Kagwa implored,
   But the skull said nothing.

The guards said, 'Kneel down.'
   They killed him with sword and spear.
Then the skull opened its mouth;
   'Huntsman, how did you come here?'
And the dead man answered,
   'Talking brought me here.'

Ian Serraillier

The Visitor

A crumbling churchyard, the sea and the moon;
The waves had gouged out grave and bone;
A man was walking, late and alone . . .

He saw a skeleton on the ground;
A ring on a bony finger he found.

He ran home to his wife and gave her the ring.
'Oh, where did you get?' He said not a thing.

'It's the loveliest ring in the world,' she said,
As it glowed on her finger. They slipped off to bed.

At midnight they woke. In the dark outside,
'Give me my ring!' a chill voice cried.

'What was that, William? What did it say?'
'Don't worry, my dear. It'll soon go away.'

'I'm coming!' A skeleton opened the door.
'Give me my ring!' It was crossing the floor.

'What was that, William? What did it say?'
'Don't worry, my dear. It'll soon go away.'

'I'm reaching you now! I'm climbing the bed.'
The wife pulled the sheet right over her head.

It was torn from her grasp and tossed in the air:
'I'll drag you out of bed by the hair!'

'What was that, William? What did it say?'
'Throw the ring through the window! THROW IT AWAY!'

She threw it. The skeleton leapt from the sill,
Scooped up the ring and clattered downhill,
Fainter . . . and fainter . . . Then all was still.

MERVYN PEAKE

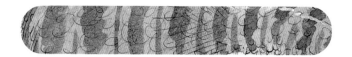

Aunts and Uncles

When Aunty Jane
Became a Crane
She put one leg behind her head;
And even when the clock struck ten
Refused to go to bed.

When Aunty Grace
Became a Plaice
She all but vanished sideways on;
Except her nose
And pointed toes
The rest of her was gone.

When Uncle Grog
Became a Dog
He hid himself for shame;
He sometimes hid his bone as well
And wouldn't hear the front-door bell,
Or answer to his name.

When Aunty Flo
Became a Crow
She had a bed put in a tree;
And there she lay
And read all day
Of ornithology.

When Aunty Vi
Became a Fly
Her favourite nephew
Sought her life;
How could he know
That with each blow
He bruised his Uncle's wife?

When Uncle Sam
Became a Ham
We did not care to carve him up;
He struggled so;
We let him go
And gave him to the pup.

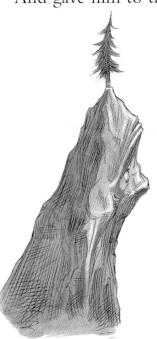

When Aunty Nag
Became a Crag
She stared across the dawn,
To where her spouse
Kept open house
With ladies on the lawn.

When Aunty Mig
Became a Pig
She floated on the briny breeze,
With irritation in her heart
And warts upon her knees.

When Aunty Jill
Became a Pill
She stared all day through dark-blue glass;
And always sneered
When men appeared
To ask her how she was.

When Uncle Jake
Became a Snake
He never found it out;
And so as no one mentions it
One sees him still about.

JOHN WALSH

The Bully Asleep

One afternoon, when grassy
Scents through the classroom crept,
Bill Craddock laid his head
Down on his desk, and slept.

The children came round him:
Jimmy, Roger, and Jane;
They lifted his head timidly
And let it sink again.

'Look, he's gone sound asleep, Miss,'
Said Jimmy Adair;
'He stays up all the night, you see;
His mother doesn't care.'

'Stand away from him, children.'
Miss Andrews stooped to see.
'Yes, he's asleep; go on
With your writing, and let him be.'

'Now's a good chance!' whispered Jimmy;
And he snatched Bill's pen and hid it.
'Kick him under the desk, hard;
He won't know who did it.'

'Fill all his pockets with rubbish –
Paper, apple-cores, chalk.'
So they plotted, while Jane
Sat wide-eyed at their talk.

Not caring, not hearing,
Bill Craddock he slept on;
Lips parted, eyes closed –
Their cruelty gone.

'Stick him with pins!' muttered Roger.
'Ink down his neck!' said Jim.
But Jane, tearful and foolish,
Wanted to comfort him.

NORMAN MacCaig

Blind Horse

He snuffles towards
pouches of water in the grass
and doesn't drink
when he finds them.

He twitches listlessly
at sappy grass stems and stands
stone still, his hanging head
caricatured with a scribble
of green whiskers.

Sometimes that head swings high,
ears cock – and he stares
down a long sound,
he stares and whinnies
for what never comes.

His eyes never close,
not in the heat of the day
when his leather lip droops and
he wears blinkers of flies.

At any time of the night
you hear him in his dark field
stamp the ground, stamp
the world down, waiting impatiently
for the light to break.

MARGARET WISE BROWN

The Secret Song

Who saw the petals
  drop from the rose?
I, said the spider,
But nobody knows.

Who saw the sunset
  flash on a bird?
I, said the fish,
But nobody heard.

Who saw the fog
    come over the sea?
I, said the sea pigeon,
Only me.

Who saw the first
    green light of the sun?
I, said the night owl,
The only one.

Who saw the moss
    creep over the stone?
I, said the gray fox,
All alone.

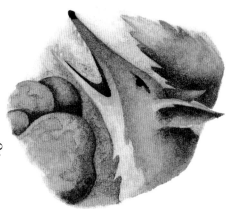

JAMES REEVES

Spells

I dance and dance without any feet –
This is the spell of the ripening wheat.

With never a tongue I've a tale to tell –
This is the meadow-grasses' spell.

I give you health without any fee –
This is the spell of the apple-tree.

I rhyme and riddle without any book –
This is the spell of the bubbling brook.

Without any legs I run for ever –
This is the spell of the mighty river.

I fall for ever and not at all –
This is the spell of the waterfall.

Without a voice I roar aloud –
This is the spell of the thunder-cloud.

No button or seam has my white coat –
This is the spell of the leaping goat.

I can cheat strangers with never a word –
This is the spell of the cuckoo-bird.

We have tongues in plenty but speak no names –
This is the spell of the fiery flames.

The creaking door has a spell to riddle –
I play a tune without any fiddle.

Rabbit and Lark

'Under the ground
    It's rumbly and dark
And interesting,'
    Said Rabbit to Lark.

Said Lark to Rabbit,
    'Up in the sky
There's plenty of room
    And it's airy and high.'

'Under the ground
    It's warm and dry.
Won't you live with me?'
    Was Rabbit's reply.

'The air's so sunny.
    I wish you'd agree,'
Said the little Lark,
    'To live with me.'

But under the ground
    And up in the sky,
Larks can't burrow
    Nor rabbits fly.

So Skylark over
    And Rabbit under
They had to settle
    To live asunder.

And often these two friends
    Meet with a will
For a chat together
    On top of the hill.

THEODORE ROETHKE

My Papa's Waltz

The whisky on your breath
Could make a small boy dizzy;
But I hung on like death:
Such waltzing was not easy.

We romped until the pans
Slid from the kitchen shelf;
My mother's countenance
Could not unfrown itself.

The hand that held my wrist
Was battered on one knuckle;
At every step you missed
My right ear scraped a buckle.

You beat time on my head
With a palm caked hard by dirt,
Then waltzed me off to bed
Still clinging to your shirt.

KATHLEEN RAINE

Spell of Creation

Within the flower there lies a seed,
In the seed there springs a tree,
In the tree there spreads a wood.

In the wood there burns a fire,
And in the fire there melts a stone,
Within the stone a ring of iron.

Within the ring there lies an O,
In the O there looks an eye,
In the eye there swims a sea,

And in the sea reflected sky,
And in the sky there shines the sun,
In the sun a bird of gold.

In the bird there beats a heart,
And from the heart there flows a song,
And in the song there sings a word.

In the word there speaks a world,
A word of joy, a word of grief,
From joy and grief there springs my love.

Oh love, my love, there springs a world,
And on the world there shines a sun,
And in the sun there burns a fire.

In the fire consumes my heart,
And in my heart there beats a bird,
And in the bird there wakes an eye,

Within the eye, earth, sea and sky,
Earth, sky and sea within an O,
Lie like the seeds within the flower.

W. H. Auden

Night Mail
(Commentary for a GPO Film)

This is the Night Mail crossing the Border,
Bringing the cheque and the postal order,

Letters for the rich, letters for the poor,
The shop at the corner, the girl next door.

Pulling up Beattock, a steady climb:
The gradient's against her, but she's on time.

Past cotton-grass and moorland boulder,
Shovelling white steam over her shoulder,

Snorting noisily, she passes
Silent miles of wind-bent grasses.

Birds turn their heads as she approaches,
Stare from bushes at her blank-faced coaches.

Sheep-dogs cannot turn her course;
They slumber on with paws across.

In the farm she passes no one wakes,
But a jug in a bedroom gently shakes.

II

Dawn freshens. Her climb is done.
Down towards Glasgow she descends,
Towards the steam tugs yelping down a glade of cranes,
Towards the fields of apparatus, the furnaces
Set on the dark plain like gigantic chessmen.
All Scotland waits for her:
In dark glens, beside pale-green lochs,
Men long for news.

III

Letters of thanks, letters from banks,
Letters of joy from girl and boy,
Receipted bills and invitations
To inspect new stock or to visit relations,
And applications for situations,
And timid lovers' declarations,
And gossip, gossip from all the nations,

News circumstantial, news financial,
Letters with holiday snaps to enlarge in,
Letters with faces scrawled on the margin,
Letters from uncles, cousins and aunts,
Letters to Scotland from the South of France,
Letters of condolence to Highlands and Lowlands,
Written on paper of every hue,
The pink, the violet, the white and the blue,
The chatty, the catty, the boring, the adoring,
The cold and official and the heart's outpouring,
Clever, stupid, short and long,
The typed and the printed and the spelt all wrong.

IV

Thousands are still asleep,
Dreaming of terrifying monsters
Or a friendly tea beside the band in Cranston's or Crawford's:
Asleep in working Glasgow, asleep in well-set Edinburgh,
Asleep in granite Aberdeen,
They continue their dreams,
But shall wake soon and hope for letters,
And none will hear the postman's knock
Without a quickening of the heart.
For who can bear to feel himself forgotten?

LYDIA PENDER

Giants

How would *you* like it –
Supposing that *you* were a snail,
And your eyes grew out on threads,
Gentle, and small, and frail –
If an enormous creature,
Reaching almost up to the distant skies,
Leaned down, and with his great finger touched your eyes
Just for the fun
Of seeing you snatch them suddenly in
And cower, quivering, back
Into your pitiful shell, so brittle and thin?
Would you think it was fun then?
Would you think it was fun?

And how would *you* like it,
Supposing you were a frog,
An emerald scrap with a pale, trembling throat
In a cool and shadowed bog,
If a tremendous monster,
Tall, tall, so that his head seemed lost in mist,
Leaned over, and clutched you up in his great fist
Just for the joy
Of watching you jump, scramble, tumble, fall,
In graceless, shivering dread,
Back into the trampled reeds that were grown so tall?
Would you think it a joy then?
Would you think it a joy?

SIR JOHN BETJEMAN

Diary of a Church Mouse
(Lines, written to order on a set subject, to be spoken on the wireless.)

Here among long-discarded cassocks,
Damp stools, and half-split open hassocks,
Here where the Vicar never looks
I nibble through old service books.
Lean and alone I spend my days
Behind this Church of England baize.
I share my dark forgotten room
With two oil-lamps and half a broom.
The cleaner never bothers me,
So here I eat my frugal tea.
My bread is sawdust mixed with straw;
My jam is polish for the floor.
　Christmas and Easter may be feasts
For congregations and for priests,
And so may Whitsun. All the same,
They do not fill my meagre frame.
For me the only feast at all
Is Autumn's Harvest Festival,
When I can satisfy my want

With ears of corn around the font.
I climb the eagle's brazen head
To burrow through a loaf of bread.
I scramble up the pulpit stair
And gnaw the marrows hanging there.
    It is enjoyable to taste
These items ere they go to waste,
But how annoying when one finds
That other mice with pagan minds
Come into church my food to share
Who have no proper business there.
Two field mice who have no desire
To be baptized, invade the choir.
A large and most unfriendly rat
Comes in to see what we are at.
He says he thinks there is no God
And yet he comes . . . it's rather odd.
This year he stole a sheaf of wheat
(It screened our special preacher's seat),
And prosperous mice from fields away
Come in to hear the organ play,
And under cover of its notes
Ate through the altar's sheaf of oats.
A Low Church mouse, who thinks that I
Am too papistical, and High,
Yet somehow doesn't think it wrong
To munch through Harvest Evensong,
While I, who starve the whole year through,
Must share my food with rodents who
Except at this time of the year

Not once inside the church appear.
  Within the human world I know
Such goings-on could not be so,
For human beings only do
What their religion tells them to.
They read the Bible every day
And always, night and morning, pray,
And just like me, the good church mouse,
Worship each week in God's own house.
  But all the same it's strange to me
How very full the church can be
With people I don't see at all
Except at Harvest Festival.

LEONARD CLARK

Good Company

I sleep in a room at the top of the house
With a flea, and a fly, and a soft-scratching mouse,
And a spider that hangs by a thread from the ceiling,
Who gives me each day such a curious feeling
When I watch him at work on the beautiful weave
Of his web that's so fine I can hardly believe
It won't all end up in such terrible tangles,
For he sways as he weaves, and spins as he dangles.
I cannot get up to that spider, I know,
And I hope he won't get down to me here below,
And yet when I wake in the chill morning air
I'd miss him if he were not still swinging there,
For I have in my room such good company,
There's him, and the mouse, and the fly, and the flea.

A. L. ROWSE

The White Cat of Trenarren
(for Beryl Cloke)

He was a mighty hunter in his youth
At Polmear all day on the mound, on the pounce
For anything moving, rabbit or bird or mouse –
  My cat and I grow old together.

After a day's hunting he'd come into the house
Delicate ears stuck all with fleas.
At Trenarren I've heard him sigh with pleasure
After a summer's day in the long-grown leas –
  My cat and I grow old together.

When I was a child I played all day,
With only a little cat for companion,
At solitary games of my own invention
Under the table or up in the green bay –
  My cat and I grow old together.

When I was a boy I wandered the roads
Up to the downs by gaunt Carn Grey,
Wrapt in a dream at end of day,
All round me the moor, below me the bay –
  My cat and I grow old together.

Now we are too often apart, yet
Turning out of Central Park into the Plaza,
Or walking Michigan Avenue against the lake-wind,
I see a little white shade in the shrubbery
Of far-off Trenarren, never far from my mind –
  My cat and I grow old together.

When I come home from too much travelling,
Cautiously he comes out of his lair to my call,
Receives me at first with a shy reproach
At long absence to him incomprehensible –
  My cat and I grow old together.

Incapable of much or long resentment,
He scratches at my door to be let out
In early morning in the ash moonlight,
Or red dawn breaking through Mother Bond's spinney –
  My cat and I grow old together.

No more frisking as of old,
Or chasing his shadow over the lawn,
But a dignified old person, tickling
His nose against twig or flower in the border,
Until evening falls and bed-time's in order,
Unable to keep eyes open any longer
He waits for me to carry him upstairs
To nestle all night snug at foot of bed –
  My cat and I grow old together.

Careful of his licked and polished appearance,
Ears like shell–whorls pink and transparent,
White plume waving proudly over the paths,
Against a background of sea and blue hydrangeas –
  My cat and I grow old together.

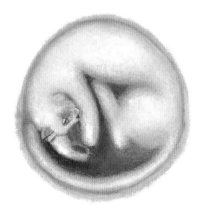

STEVIE SMITH

The Old Sweet Dove of Wiveton

'Twas the voice of the sweet dove
I heard him move,
I heard him cry:
Love, love.

High in the chestnut tree
Is the nest of the old dove
And there he sits solitary
Crying, Love, love.

The gray of this heavy day
Makes the green of the tree's leaves and the grass brighter,
And the flowers of the chestnut tree whiter,
And whiter the flowers of the high cow-parsley.

So still is the air,
So heavy the sky,
You can hear the splash
Of the water falling from the green grass
As Red and Honey push by,
The old dogs,
Gone away, gone hunting by the marsh bogs.

Happy the retriever dogs in their pursuit,
Happy in bog-mud the busy foot.

Now all is silent, it is silent again,
In the sombre day and the beginning soft rain,
It is a silence made more actual
By the moan from the high tree that is occasional.

Where in his nest above
Still sits the old dove,
Murmuring solitary,
Crying for pain,
Crying most melancholy
Again and again.

OGDEN NASH

The Wombat

The wombat lives across the seas,
Among the far Antipodes.
He may exist on nuts and berries,
Or then again, on missionaries;
His distant habitat precludes
Conclusive knowledge of his moods.
But I would not engage the wombat
In any form of mortal combat.

The Purist

I give you now Professor Twist,
A conscientious scientist.
Trustees exclaimed, 'He never bungles!'
And sent him off to distant jungles.
Camped on a tropic riverside,
One day he missed his living bride.
She had, the guide informed him later,
Been eaten by an alligator.
Professor Twist could not but smile.
'You mean,' he said, 'a crocodile.'

ROBERT GRAVES

The Alice Jean

One moonlight night a ship drove in,
   A ghost ship from the west,
Drifting with bare mast and lone tiller;
   Like a mermaid drest
In long green weed and barnacles
   She beached and came to rest.

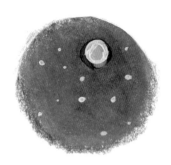

All the watchers of the coast
   Flocked to view the sight;
Men and women, streaming down
   Through the summer night,
Found her standing tall and ragged
   Beached in the moonlight.

Then one old woman stared aghast:
   'The *Alice Jean*? But no!
The ship that took my Ned from me
   Sixty years ago –
Drifted back from the utmost west
   With the ocean's flow?

'Caught and caged in the weedy pool
   Beyond the western brink,
Where crewless vessels lie and rot
   In waters black as ink,
Torn out at last by a sudden gale –
   Is it the *Jean*, you think?'

   A hundred women gaped at her,
    The menfolk nudged and laughed,
   But none could find a likelier story
    For the strange craft
   With fear and death and desolation
    Rigged fore and aft.

The blind ship came forgotten home
   To all but one of these,
Of whom none dared to climb aboard her:
   And by and by the breeze
Veered hard about, and the *Alice Jean*
   Foundered in foaming seas.

The Penny Fiddle

Yesterday I bought a penny fiddle
  And put it to my chin to play,
But I found that the strings were painted,
  So I threw my fiddle away.

A gipsy girl found my penny fiddle
  As it lay abandoned there;
When she asked me if she might keep it,
  I told her I did not care.

Then she drew such music from the fiddle
  With help of a farthing bow,
That I offered five shillings for the secret.
  But, alas, she would not let it go.

RACHEL FIELD

Something Told the Wild Geese

Something told the wild geese
    It was time to go.
Though the field lay golden
    Something whispered, 'Snow.'
Leaves were green and stirring,
    Berries, lustre-glossed,
But beneath warm feathers
    Something cautioned, 'Frost.'
All the sagging orchards
    Steamed with amber spice,
But each wild breast stiffened
    At remembered ice.
Something told the wild geese
    It was time to fly –
Summer sun was on their wings,
    Winter in their cry.

E. E. Cummings

maggie and milly and molly and may

maggie and milly and molly and may
went down to the beach (to play one day)

and maggie discovered a shell that sang
so sweetly she couldn't remember her troubles, and

milly befriended a stranded star
whose rays five languid fingers were;

and molly was chased by a horrible thing
which raced sideways while blowing bubbles: and

may came home with a smooth round stone
as small as a world and as large as alone.

For whatever we lose (like a you or a me)
it's always ourselves we find in the sea

ELIZABETH COATSWORTH

Song of the Rabbits Outside the Tavern

We who play under the pines,
we who dance in the snow
that shines blue in the light of the moon
sometimes halt as we go,
stand with our ears erect,
our noses testing the air,
to gaze at the golden world
behind the windows there.

Suns they have in a cave
and stars each on a tall white stem,
and the thought of fox or night owl
seems never to trouble them.
They laugh and eat and are warm,
their food seems ready at hand,
while hungry out in the cold
we little rabbits stand.

But they never dance as we dance,
they have not the speed nor the grace.
We scorn both the cat and the dog
who lie by their fireplace.
We scorn them licking their paws,
their eyes on an upraised spoon,
we who dance hungry and wild
under a winter's moon.

WILFRED OWEN

Extract from The Little Mermaid

Far out at sea, the water is as blue
As cornflowers, and as clear as crystal-core;
But so exceeding deep, no sea-bird's view
Can fathom it, nor men's ropes touch its floor.
Strange, snake-like trees and weeds – the same which grew
Before dry land with herbs was peopled o'er –
Still sleep in heavy peacefulness down there,
And hold their fluctuous arms towards upper air.

And it is there the Sea-King's nation dwells.
His palace, golden-bright and ruby-red,
Gleams like a crown among those velvet dells.
Pink, shimmering streams of light its windows shed,
Like waterfalls of wine; and pink-white shells,
Like Alpine snows, its lofty roof o'erspread;
Which close and open, close and open wide,
With every ebb and flowing of the tide.

W. J. TURNER

India

They hunt, the velvet tigers in the jungle,
The spotted jungle full of shapeless patches –
Sometimes they're leaves, sometimes they're hanging flowers,
Sometimes they're hot gold patches of the sun:
They hunt, the velvet tigers in the jungle!

What do they hunt by glimmering pools of water,
By the round silver Moon, the Pool of Heaven –
In the striped grass, amid the barkless trees –
The stars scattered like eyes of beasts above them!

What do they hunt, their hot breath scorching insects,
Insects that blunder blindly in the way,
Vividly fluttering – they also are hunting,
Are glittering with a tiny ecstasy!

The grass is flaming and the trees are growing,
The very mud is gurgling in the pools,
Green toads are watching, crimson parrots flying,
Two pairs of eyes meet one another glowing –
They hunt, the velvet tigers in the jungle.

T. S. ELIOT

Skimbleshanks: The Railway Cat

There's a whisper down the line at 11.39
When the Night Mail's ready to depart,
Saying 'Skimble where is Skimble has he gone to hunt the
                                                  thimble?
We must find him or the train can't start.'
All the guards and all the porters and the stationmaster's
                                                  daughters
They are searching high and low,
Saying 'Skimble where is Skimble for unless he's very nimble
Then the Night Mail just can't go.'
At 11.42 then the signal's overdue
And the passengers are frantic to a man –
Then Skimble will appear and he'll saunter to the rear:
He's been busy in the luggage van!
   He gives one flash of his glass-green eyes
      And the signal goes 'All Clear!'
   And we're off at last for the northern part
      Of the Northern Hemisphere!
You may say that by and large it is Skimble who's in charge
Of the Sleeping Car Express.
From the driver and the guards to the bagmen playing cards
He will supervise them all, more or less.

Down the corridor he paces and examines all the faces
Of the travellers in the First and in the Third;
He establishes control by a regular patrol
And he'd know at once if anything occurred.
He will watch you without winking and he sees what you are
thinking

And it's certain that he doesn't approve
Of hilarity and riot, so the folk are very quiet
When Skimble is about and on the move.
   You can play no pranks with Skimbleshanks!
      He's a Cat that cannot be ignored;
   So nothing goes wrong on the Northern Mail
      When Skimbleshanks is aboard.
Oh it's very pleasant when you have found your little den
With your name written up on the door.
And the berth is very neat with a newly folded sheet
And there's not a speck of dust on the floor.
There is every sort of light – you can make it dark or bright:
There's a button that you turn to make a breeze.
There's a funny little basin you're supposed to wash your face in
And a crank to shut the window if you sneeze.
Then the guard looks in politely and will ask you very brightly
'Do you like your morning tea weak or strong?'
But Skimble's just behind him and was ready to remind him,
For Skimble won't let anything go wrong.
   And when you creep into your cosy berth
      And pull up the counterpane,
   You ought to reflect that it's very nice
   To know that you won't be bothered by mice –
   You can leave all that to the Railway Cat,

The Cat of the Railway Train!
In the watches of the night he is always fresh and bright;
Every now and then he has a cup of tea
With perhaps a drop of Scotch while he's keeping on the watch,
Only stopping here and there to catch a flea.
You were fast asleep at Crewe and so you never knew
That he was walking up and down the station;
You were sleeping all the while he was busy at Carlisle,
Where he greets the stationmaster with elation.
But you saw him at Dumfries, where he summons the police
If there's anything they ought to know about:
When you get to Gallowgate there you do not have to wait –
For Skimbleshanks will help you to get out!
He gives you a wave of his long brown tail
Which says: 'I'll see you again!
You'll meet without fail on the Midnight Mail
The Cat of the Railway Train.'

RUPERT BROOKE

These I Have Loved . . .

These I have loved:
       White plates and cups, clean-gleaming,
Ringed with blue lines; and feathery, faery dust;
Wet roofs, beneath the lamp-light; the strong crust
Of friendly bread; and many-tasting food;
Rainbows; and the blue bitter smoke of wood;
And radiant raindrops couching in cool flowers;
And flowers themselves, that sway through sunny hours,
Dreaming of moths that drink them under the moon;
Then, the cool kindliness of sheets, that soon
Smooth away trouble; and the rough male kiss
Of blankets; grainy wood; live hair that is
Shining and free; blue-massing clouds; the keen
Unpassioned beauty of a great machine;
The benison of hot water; furs to touch;
The good smell of old clothes; and other such –
The comfortable smell of friendly fingers,
Hair's fragrance, and the musty reek that lingers
About dead leaves and last year's ferns . . .

                              Dear names,
And thousand other throng to me! Royal flames;
Sweet water's dimpling laugh from tap or spring;
Holes in the ground; and voices that do sing;
Voices in laughter, too; and body's pain,
Soon turned to peace; and the deep-panting train;
Firm sands; the little dulling edge of foam
That browns and dwindles as the wave goes home;
And washen stones, gay for an hour; the cold
Graveness of iron; moist black earthen mould;
Sleep; and high places; footprints in the dew;
And oaks; and brown horse-chestnuts, glossy-new;
And new-peeled sticks; and shining pools on grass;
All these have been my loves.

E. V. RIEU

Sir Smashum Uppe

Good afternoon, Sir Smashum Uppe!
We're having tea: do take a cup!
Sugar and milk? Now let me see –
Two lumps, I think? . . . Good gracious me!
The silly thing slipped off your knee!
Pray don't apologize, old chap:
A very trivial mishap!
So clumsy of you? How absurd!
My dear Sir Smashum, not a word!
Now do sit down and have another,
And tell us all about your brother –
You know, the one who broke his head.
Is the poor fellow still in bed?
A chair – allow me, sir! . . . Great Scott!
That was a nasty smash! Eh, what?
Oh, not at all: the chair was old –
Queen Anne, or so we have been told.
We've got at least a dozen more:
Just leave the pieces on the floor.
I want you to admire our view:
Come nearer to the window, do;
And look how beautiful . . . Tut, tut!

You didn't see that it was shut?
I hope you are not badly cut!
Not hurt? A fortunate escape!
Amazing! Not a single scrape!
And now, if you have finished tea,
I fancy you might like to see
A little thing or two I've got.
That china plate? Yes, worth a lot:
A beauty too . . . Ah, there it goes!
I trust it didn't hurt your toes?
Your elbow brushed it off the shelf?
Of course: I've done the same myself.
And now, my dear Sir Smashum – Oh,
You surely don't intend to go?
You *must* be off? Well, come again,
So glad you're fond of porcelain.

A. A. MILNE

Lines and Squares

Whenever I walk in a London street,
I'm ever so careful to watch my feet;
    And I keep in the squares,
    And the masses of bears,
Who wait at the corners all ready to eat
The sillies who tread on the lines of the street,
    Go back to their lairs,
  And I say to them, 'Bears,
Just look how I'm walking in all the squares!'

And the little bears growl to each other, 'He's mine,
As soon as he's silly and steps on a line.'

And some of the bigger bears try to pretend
That they came round the corner to look for a friend;
And they try to pretend that nobody cares
Whether you walk on the lines or squares.
But only the sillies believe their talk;
It's ever so portant how you walk.

And it's ever so jolly to call out, 'Bears,
Just watch me walking in all the squares!'

Daffodowndilly

She wore her yellow sun-bonnet,
  She wore her greenest gown;
She turned to the south wind
  And curtsied up and down.
She turned to the sunlight
  And shook her yellow head,
And whispered to her neighbour:
  'Winter is dead.'

ELEANOR FARJEON

The Distance

Over the sounding sea,
Off the wandering sea
I smelt the smell of the distance
And longed for another existence.
Smell of pineapple, maize, and myrrh,
Parrot-feather and monkey-fur,
  Brown spice,
  Blue ice,
Fields of tobacco and tea and rice,
  And soundless snows,
  And snowy cotton,
  Otto of rose
Incense in an ivory palace,
Jungle rivers rich and rotten,
  Slumbering valleys,
  Smouldering mountains,
  Rank morasses
  And frozen fountains,
Black molasses and purple wine,
Coral and pearl and tar and brine,
The smell of panther and polar-bear
  And leopard-lair

And mermaid-hair
Came from the four-cornered distance,
And I longed for another existence.

The Sounds in the Evening

The sounds in the evening
Go all through the house,
The click of the clock
And the pick of the mouse,
The footsteps of people
Upon the top floor,
The skirts of my mother
That brush by my door,
The crick in the boards,
And the creak of the chairs,
The fluttering murmurs
Outside on the stairs,
The ring at the bell,
The arrival of guests,
The laugh of my father
At one of his jests,
The clashing of dishes
As dinner goes in,
The babble of voices
That distance makes thin,

The mewings of cats
That seem just by my ear,
The hooting of owls
That can never seem near,
The queer little noises
That no one explains –
Till the moon through the slats
Of my window-blind rains,
And the world of my eyes
And my ears melts like steam
As I find in my pillow
The world of my dream.

VACHEL LINDSAY

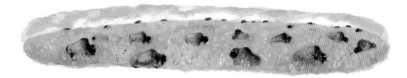

The Flower-Fed Buffaloes

The flower-fed buffaloes of the spring
In the days of long ago,
Ranged where the locomotives sing
And the prairie flowers lie low;
The tossing, blooming, perfumed grass
Is swept away by wheat,
Wheels and wheels and wheels spin by
In the spring that still is sweet.
But the flower-fed buffaloes of the spring
Left us long ago.
They gore no more, they bellow no more,
They trundle around the hills no more:
With the Blackfeet, lying low,
With the Pawnees, lying low.

JOHN MASEFIELD

An Old Song Re-Sung

I saw a ship a-sailing, a-sailing, a-sailing,
With emeralds and rubies and sapphires in her hold;
And a bosun in a blue coat bawling at the railing,
Piping through a silver call that had a chain of gold;
The summer wind was failing and the tall ship rolled.

I saw a ship a-steering, a-steering, a-steering,
With roses in red thread worked upon her sails;
With sacks of purple amethysts, the spoils of buccaneering,
Skins of musky yellow wine, and silks in bales,
Her merry men were cheering, hauling on the brails.

I saw a ship a-sinking, a-sinking, a-sinking,
With glittering sea-water splashing on her decks,
With seamen in her spirit-room singing songs and drinking,
Pulling claret bottles down, and knocking off the necks,
The broken glass was chinking as she sank among the wrecks.

EDWARD THOMAS

Snow

In the gloom of whiteness,
In the great silence of snow,
A child was sighing
And bitterly saying: 'Oh,
They have killed a white bird up there on her nest,
The down is fluttering from her breast!'
And still it fell through the dusky brightness
On the child crying for the bird of the snow.

ROBERT SERVICE

The Cremation of Sam McGee

There are strange things done in the midnight sun
* By the men who moil for gold;*
The Arctic trails have their secret tales
* That would make your blood run cold;*
The Northern Lights have seen queer sights,
* But the queerest they ever did see*
Was that night on the marge of Lake Lebarge
* I cremated Sam McGee.*

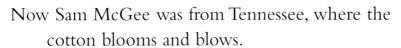

Now Sam McGee was from Tennessee, where the
    cotton blooms and blows.
Why he left his home in the South to roam 'round the
    Pole, God only knows.
He was always cold, but the land of gold seemed to
    hold him like a spell;
Though he'd often say in his homely way that 'he'd
    sooner live in hell.'

On a Christmas Day we were mushing our way over
the Dawson trail.
Talk of your cold! through the parka's fold it stabbed
like a driven nail.
If our eyes we'd close, then the lashes froze till
sometimes we couldn't see;
It wasn't much fun, but the only one to whimper was
Sam McGee.

And that very night, as we lay packed tight in our
robes beneath the snow.
And the dogs were fed, the stars o'erhead were dancing
heel and toe,
He turned to me, and 'Cap,' says he, 'I'll cash in this
trip, I guess;
And if I do, I'm asking that you won't refuse my last
request.'

Well, he seemed so low that I couldn't say no; then he
says with a sort of moan:
'It's the cursed cold, and it's got right hold till I'm
chilled clean through to the bone.
Yet 'tain't being dead – it's my awful dread of the icy
grave that pains;
So I want you to swear that, foul or fair, you'll cremate
my last remains.'

A pal's last need is a thing to heed, so I swore I would
      not fail;
And we started on at the streak of dawn; but God! he
      looked ghastly pale.
He crouched on the sleigh, and he raved all day of his
      home in Tennessee;
And before nightfall a corpse was all that was left of
      Sam McGee.

There wasn't a breath in that land of death, and I
      hurried horror-driven,
With a corpse half hid that I couldn't get rid, because
      of a promise given;
It was lashed to the sleigh, and it seemed to say: 'You
      may tax your brawn and brains,
But you promised true, and it's up to you to cremate
      those last remains.'

Now a promise made is a debt unpaid, and the trail
      has its own stern code.
In the days to come, though my lips were dumb, in
      my heart how I cursed that load.
In the long, long night, by the lone firelight, while the
      huskies, round in a ring,
Howled out their woes to the homeless snows –
      O God! how I loathed the thing.

And every day that quiet clay seemed to heavy and
  heavier grow;
And on I went, though the dogs were spent and the
  grub was getting low;
The trail was bad, and I felt half mad, but I swore I
  would not give in;
And I'd often sing to the hateful thing, and it
  hearkened with a grin.

Till I came to the marge of Lake Lebarge, and a derelict
  there lay;
It was jammed in the ice, but I saw in a trice it was
  called the 'Alice May.'
And I looked at it, and I thought a bit, and looked at
  my frozen chum;
Then 'Here,' said I, with a sudden cry, 'is my cre-ma
  tor-eum.'

Some planks I tore from the cabin floor, and I lit the
  boiler fire;
Some coal I found that was lying around, and I heaped
  the fuel higher;
The flames just soared, and the furnace roared – such a
  blaze you seldom see;
And I burrowed a hole in the glowing coal, and I
  stuffed in Sam McGee.

Then I made a hike, for I didn't like to hear him sizzle
    so;
And the heavens scowled, and the huskies howled, and
    the wind began to blow.
It was icy cold, but the hot sweat rolled down my
    cheeks, and I don't know why;
And the greasy smoke in an inky cloak went
    streaking down the sky.

I do not know how long in the snow I wrestled with
    grisly fear;
But the stars came out and they danced about ere again
    I ventured near;
I was sick with dread, but I bravely said: 'I'll just take
    a peep inside.
I guess he's cooked, and it's time I looked'; . . . then
    the door I opened wide.

And there sat Sam, looking cool and calm, in the heart
    of the furnace roar;
And he wore a smile you could see a mile, and he said:
    'Please close that door.
It's fine in here, but I greatly fear you'll let in the cold
    and storm –
Since I left Plumtree, down in Tennessee, it's the first
    time I've been warm.'

There are strange things done in the midnight sun
    By the men who moil for gold;
The Arctic trails have their secret tales
    That would make your blood run cold;
The Northern Lights have seen queer sights,
    But the queerest they ever did see
Was that night on the marge of Lake Lebarge
    I cremated Sam McGee.

HARRY GRAHAM

Politeness

My cousin John was most polite;
He led shortsighted Mrs Bond,
By accident, one winter's night
Into a village pond.
Her life perhaps he might have saved
But how genteelly he behaved!

Each time she rose and waved to him
He smiled and bowed and doffed his hat;
Thought he, although I cannot swim,
At least I can do that –
And when for the third time she sank
He stood bareheaded on the bank.

Be civil, then, to young and old;
Especially to persons who
Possess a quantity of gold
Which they might leave to you.
The more they have, it seems to me,
The more polite you ought to be.

ROBERT FROST

Stopping by Woods on a Snowy Evening

Whose woods these are I think I know.
His house is in the village, though;
He will not see me stopping here
To watch his woods fill up with snow.

My little horse must think it queer
To stop without a farmhouse near
Between the woods and frozen lake
The darkest evening of the year.

He gives his harness bells a shake
To ask if there is some mistake.
The only other sound's the sweep
Of easy wind and downy flake.

The woods are lovely, dark, and deep,
But I have promises to keep,
And miles to go before I sleep,
And miles to go before I sleep.

A Minor Bird

I have wished a bird would fly away,
And not sing by my house all day;

Have clapped my hands at him from the door
When it seemed as if I could bear no more.

The fault must partly have been in me.
The bird was not to blame for his key.

And of course there must be something wrong
In wanting to silence any song.

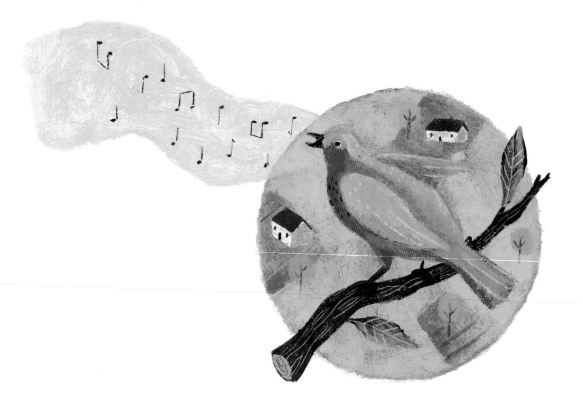

G. K. CHESTERTON

The Donkey

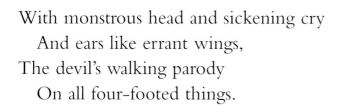

When fishes flew and forests walked,
    And figs grew upon thorn,
Some moment when the moon was blood,
    Then surely I was born;

With monstrous head and sickening cry
    And ears like errant wings,
The devil's walking parody
    On all four-footed things.

The tattered outlaw of the earth,
    Of ancient crooked will;
Starve, scourge, deride me: I am dumb,
    I keep my secret still.

Fools! For I also had my hour;
    One far fierce hour and sweet:
There was a shout about my ears,
    And palms before my feet.

WALTER DE LA MARE

Tom's Angel

No one was in the fields
But me and Polly Flint,
When, like a giant across the grass,
The flaming angel went.

It was budding time in May,
And green as green could be,
And all in his height he went along
Past Polly Flint and me.

We'd been playing in the woods,
And Polly up, and ran,
And hid her face, and said,
'Tom! Tom! The Man! The Man!'

And I up-turned; and there,
Like flames across the sky,
With wings all bristling, came
The Angel striding by.

And a chaffinch overhead
Kept whistling in the tree
While the Angel, blue as fire, came on
Past Polly Flint and me.

And I saw his hair, and all
The ruffling of his hem,
As over the clovers his bare feet
Trod without stirring them.

Polly – she cried; and, oh!
We ran, until the lane
Turned by the miller's roaring wheel,
And we were safe again.

The Scarecrow

All winter through I bow my head
   Beneath the driving rain;
The North Wind powders me with snow
   And blows me black again;
At midnight in a maze of stars
   I flame with glittering rime,
And stand, above the stubble, stiff
   As mail at morning-prime.
But when that child, called Spring, and all

His host of children, come,
Scattering their buds and dew upon
    These acres of my home,
Some rapture in my rags awakes;
    I lift void eyes and scan
The skies for crows, those ravening foes,
    Of my strange master, Man.
I watch him striding lank behind
    His clashing team, and know
Soon will the wheat swish body high
    Where once lay sterile snow;
Soon shall I gaze across a sea
    Of sun-begotten grain,
Which my unflinching watch hath sealed
    For harvest once again.

A Robin

Ghost-grey the fall of night,
    Ice-bound the lane,
Lone in the dying light
    Flits he again;
Lurking where shadows steal,
Perched in his coat of blood,
Man's homestead at his heel,
    Death-still the wood.

W. H. DAVIES

The Blind Boxer

He goes with basket and slow feet,
To sell his nuts from street to street;
The very terror of his kind,
Till blackened eyes had made him blind.
For this is Boxer Bob, the man
That had hard muscles, harder than
A schoolboy's bones; who held his ground
When six tall bullies sparred around.
Small children now, that have no grace,
Can steal his nuts before his face;
And when he threatens with his hands,
Mock him two feet from where he stands;
Mock him who could some years ago
Have leapt five feet to strike a blow.
Poor Bobby, I remember when
Thou wert a god to drunken men;
But now they push thee off, or crack
Thy nuts and give no money back.
They swear they'll strike thee in the face,
Dost thou not hurry from that place.
Such are the men that once would pay
To keep thee drunk from day to day.

With all thy strength and cunning skill,
Thy courage, lasting breath and will,
Thou'rt helpless now; a little ball,
No bigger than a cherry small,
Has now refused to guide and lead
Twelve stone of strong hard flesh that need
But that ball's light to make thee leap
And strike these cowards down like sheep.
Poor helpless Bobby, blind; I see
Thy working face and pity thee.

The Happy Child

I saw this day sweet flowers grow thick –
But not one like the child did pick.

I heard the pack-hounds in green park –
But no dog like the child heard bark.

I heard this day bird after bird –
But not one like the child has heard.

A hundred butterflies saw I –
But not one like the child saw fly.

I saw the horses roll in grass –
But no horse like the child saw pass.

My world this day has lovely been –
But not like what the child has seen.

Hilaire Belloc

The Vulture

The Vulture eats between his meals,
    And that's the reason why
He very, very rarely feels
    As well as you or I.
His eye is dull, his head is bald,
    His neck is growing thinner.
Oh, what a lesson for us all
    To only eat at dinner.

The Frog

Be kind and tender to the Frog,
　And do not call him names,
As 'Slimy-skin', or 'Polly-wog',
　Or likewise 'Uncle James',
Or 'Gape-a-grin', or 'Toad-gone-wrong',
　Or 'Billy-Bandy Knees':
The frog is justly sensitive
　To epithets like these.

No animal will more repay
　A treatment kind and fair,
At least so lonely people say
Who keep a frog (and by the way,
　They are extremely rare).

MARY GILMORE

The Wild Horses

Let the dark mountain shake to the thunder
  Where the wild horses trample the fern,
Let the deep vales re-echo and wonder,
  When, like an eddy, they circle and turn!
Watch the lithe motion
Run free as an ocean,
Never has man laid a hand on a head;
Never a halter
Had bid a step falter,
Never a crest bent down to be led!

Mark, in their starting, the pride of their bearing.
  Swift wheel the leaders, each in his place;
Snorting, they stare at us, timid and daring,
  Ere with a whirl they are off at a race.
O, the wild sally,
As, down through the valley,
Turn they again to the mountains they know;
Chased and the chaser
Outstretched like a racer,
Where, as the wind, unconquered they go! . . .

What though the pommel scarce keep you from reeling;
   What though the breath be almost a cry;
What though all turn in a dream that is stealing
   Sense from intention and light from the eye –
Follow them, follow,
By height and by hollow;
Follow them, follow, whatever the course!
Soon will the wonder
Die out with the thunder,
Soon will the mountain forget the wild horse.

W. B. YEATS

The Song of Wandering Aengus

I went out to the hazel wood,
Because a fire was in my head,
And cut and peeled a hazel wand,
And hooked a berry to a thread;
And when white moths were on the wing,
And moth-like stars were flickering out,
I dropped the berry in a stream
And caught a little silver trout.

When I laid it on the floor
I went to blow the fire aflame,
But something rustled on the floor,
And someone called me by my name.
It had become a glimmering girl
With apple blossom in her hair
Who called me by my name and ran
And faded through the brightening air.

Though I am old with wandering
Through hollow lands and hilly lands,
I will find out where she has gone,
And kiss her lips and take her hands;
And walk among long dappled grass,
And pluck till time and times are done
The silver apples of the moon,
The golden apples of the sun.

RUDYARD KIPLING

A Smuggler's Song

If you wake at midnight and hear a horse's feet,
Don't go drawing back the blind, or looking in the street,
Them that asks no questions isn't told a lie.
Watch the wall, my darling, while the Gentlemen go by!
      Five and twenty ponies,
      Trotting through the dark –
      Brandy for the Parson,
      Baccy for the Clerk;
      Laces for a lady; letters for a spy,
And watch the wall, my darling, while the Gentlemen go by!

Running round the woodlump if you chance to find
Little barrels, roped and tarred, all full of brandy-wine;
Don't you shout to come and look, nor take 'em for your play;
Put the brushwood back again, – and they'll be gone next day!

If you see the stableyard setting open wide;
If you see a tired horse lying down inside;
If your mother mends a coat cut about and tore;
If the lining's wet and warm – don't you ask no more!

If you meet King George's men, dressed in blue and red,
You be careful what you say, and mindful what is said.
If they call you 'pretty maid', and chuck you 'neath the chin,
Don't you tell where no one is, nor yet where no one's been!

Knocks and footsteps round the house – whistles after dark –
You've no call for running out till the housedogs bark.
Trusty's here and Pincher's here, and see how dumb they lie –
They don't fret to follow when the Gentlemen go by!

If you do as you've been told, likely there's a chance,
You'll be give a dainty doll, – all the way from France,
With a cap of Valenciennes, and a velvet hood –
A present from the Gentlemen, along o' being good!
      Five and twenty ponies,
      Trotting through the dark –
      Brandy for the Parson,
      Baccy for the Clerk;
Them that asks no questions isn't told a lie –
Watch the wall, my darling, while the Gentlemen go by!

A. B. (Banjo) Paterson

Waltzing Matilda

Oh! there once was a swagman camped by a Billabong
   Under the shade of a Coolabah tree;
And he sang as he looked at his old billy boiling,
   'Who'll come a-waltzing Matilda with me?'

Who'll come a-waltzing Matilda, my darling,
   Who'll come a-waltzing Matilda with me?
Waltzing Matilda and leading a water-bag —
   Who'll come a-waltzing Matilda with me?

Down came a jumbuck to drink at the water-hole,
   Up jumped the swagman and grabbed him in glee;
And he sang as he stowed him away in his tucker-bag,
   'You'll come a-waltzing Matilda with me!'

Down came the Squatter a-riding his thoroughbred;
   Down came Policemen – one, two, and three.
'Whose is the jumbuck you've got in the tucker-bag?
   You'll come a-waltzing Matilda with me.'

But the swagman, he up and he jumped in the water hole,
    Drowning himself by the Coolabah tree;
And his ghost may be heard as it sings in the Billabong,
    'Who'll come a-waltzing Matilda with me?'

A. E. HOUSMAN

When Green Buds Hang

When green buds hang in the elm like dust
   And sprinkle the lime like rain,
Forth I wander, forth I must,
   And drink of life again.
Forth I must by hedgerow bowers
   To look at the leaves uncurled,
And stand in the fields where cuckoo-flowers
   Are lying about the world.

KATHERINE PYLE

The Toys Talk of the World

'I should like,' said the vase from the china-store,
'To have seen the world a little more.

'When they carried me here I was wrapped up tight,
But they say it is really a lovely sight.'

'Yes,' said a little plaster bird,
'That is exactly what I have heard;

'There are thousands of trees, and oh, what a sight
It must be when the candles are all alight.'

The fat top rolled on his other side:
'It is not in the least like that,' he cried.

'Except myself and the kite and ball,
None of you know of the world at all.

'There are houses, and pavements hard and red,
And everything spins around,' he said;

'Sometimes it goes slowly, and sometimes fast,
And often it stops with a bump at last.'

The wooden donkey nodded his head:
'I had heard the world was like that,' he said.

The kite and the ball exchanged a smile,
But they did not speak; it was not worth while.

THOMAS HARDY

Snow in the Suburbs

Every branch big with it,
Bent every twig with it;
Every fork like a white web-foot;
Every street and pavement mute:
Some flakes have lost their way, and grope back upward, when
Meeting those meandering down they turn and descend again.
The palings are glued together like a wall,
And there is no waft of wind with the fleecy fall.

A sparrow enters the tree,
Whereon immediately
A snow-lump thrice his own slight size
Descends on him and showers his head and eyes,
And overturns him,
And near inurns him,
And lights on a nether twig, when its brush
Starts off a volley of other lodging lumps with a rush.

The steps are a blanched slope,
Up which, with feeble hope,
A black cat comes, wide-eyed and thin;
And we take him in.

Transformations

Portion of this yew
Is a man my grandsire knew,
Bosomed here at its foot:
This branch may be his wife,
A ruddy human life
Now turned to a green shoot.

These grasses must be made
Of her who often prayed
Last century, for repose;
And the fair girl long ago
Whom I often tried to know
May be entering this rose.

So, they are not underground,
But as nerves and veins abound
In the growths of upper air,
And they feel the sun and rain,
And the energy again
That made them what they were!

INDEX OF POETS

Agard, John   7
Ahlberg, Allan   27
Auden, W. H.   92
Barker, George   71
Belloc, Hilaire   148
Berry, James   47
Betjeman, Sir John   97
Bodecker, N. M.   52
Brooke, Rupert   120
Causley, Charles   60
Chesterton, G. K.   141
Clark, Leonard   100
Coatsworth, Elizabeth   113
Cummings, E. E.   112
Dahl, Roald   63
Davies, W. H.   145
de la Mare, Walter   142
Dugan, Michael   9
Edwards, Richard   5
Eliot, T. S.   117
Farjeon, Eleanor   126
Fatchen, Max   56
Field, Rachel   111
Frost, Robert   139
Gilmore, Mary   150
Graham, Harry   138
Graves, Robert   108
Hardy, Thomas   161
Heath-Stubbs, John   57
Henri, Adrian   39
Hoberman, Mary Ann   44
Housman, A. E.   158
Houston, Libby   19
Hughes, Ted   42
Jennings, Elizabeth   46
Kipling, Rudyard   154
Larkin, Philip   51

Lee, Dennis 24
Lee, Laurie 70
Lindsay, Vachel 129
Lowbury, Edward 73
MacCaig Norman 82
McGough, Roger 29
Masefield, John 130
Merriam, Eve 66
Milligan, Spike 58
Milne, A. A. 124
Mitchell, Adrian 36
Morgan, Edwin 54
Nash, Ogden 106
Nichols, Grace 4
Owen, Gareth 32
Owen, Wilfred 115
Paterson, A. B. (Banjo) 156
Patten, Brian 14
Peake, Mervyn 77
Pender, Lydia 95
Prelutsky, Jack 21
Pyle, Katharine 159
Raine, Kathleen 90
Reeves, James 86
Rieu, E. V. 122
Roethke, Theodore 89
Rosen, Michael 10
Rowse, A. L. 101
Scannell, Vernon 49
Serraillier Ian 75
Service, Robert 132
Silverstein, Shel 40
Smith, Stevie 104
Thomas, Dylan 69
Thomas, Edward 131
Turner, W. J. 116
Walsh, John 80
Wilbur, Richard 53
Willard, Nancy 34
Wise Brown, Margaret 84
Wright, Judith 68
Wright, Kit 16
Yeats, W. B. 152
Zephaniah, Benjamin 1

Index of First Lines

A crumbling churchyard, the sea and the moon;   75
A flea flew by a bee. The bee   44
All winter through I bow my head   143
Along the road the magpies walk   68
Be kind and tender to the Frog,   149
Behold the apples' rounded worlds: 70
Billy McBone   27
Call alligator long-mouth   7
Colonel Fazackerley Butterworth-Toast   61
Dere's a Sonnet   1
Down the Holloway Road on the top of the bus   17
'Down vith children! Do them in!   63
Every branch big with it,   161
Far out at sea, the water is as blue   115
Ghost-grey the fall of night,   144
Good afternoon, Sir Smashum Uppe!   122
He gave silver shoes to the rabbit   34
He goes with basket and slow feet,   145
He snuffles towards   82
He was a mighty hunter in his youth   101
Here among long-discarded cassocks,   97
Homework! Oh, homework!   21
How would *you* like it –   95
'I cannot go to school today,'   40
I dance and dance without any feet –   86
I did a bad thing once   28
I give you now Professor Twist,   107
I have wished a bird would fly away,   140
I know a rat on Ararat   4
I met a wizened wood-woman   20
I saw a ship a-sailing, a-sailing, a-sailing,   130

I saw this day sweet flowers grow thick –	147
'I should like,' said the vase from the china-store,	159
I sleep in a room at the top of the house	100
I touched my first rose	3
I went out to the hazel wood,	152
I wish my teacher's eyes wouldn't	47
If you don't put your shoes on before I count fifteen	10
If you wake at midnight and hear a horse's feet,	154
I'm the youngest in our house	12
In a little white room	8
In the gloom of whiteness,	131
It's Susan I talk to not Tracey,	39
jollymerry	54
Kagwa hunted the lion,	73
Lady Barnaby takes her ease	58
Let the dark mountain shake to the thunder	150
Lizzy had a lion	24
Lovers lie around in it	36
Loving words clutch crimson roses	5
maggie and milly and molly and may	112
Mother, there's a strange man	29
My cousin John was most polite;	138
My name is Tom Bone,	60
My Uncle Jim-jim	58
No one was in the fields	142
'Nowhere in the world,'	52
Oh! there once was a swagman camped by a Billabong	156
On shallow straw, in shadeless glass,	51
Once upon a time	66
One afternoon, when grassy	80
One moonlight night a ship drove in,	108
Over the sounding sea,	126
Portion of this yew	163
Pussycat, pussycat, where have you been,	56
She wore her yellow sun-bonnet,	125
Sleep, my baby, the night is coming soon.	46
Something told the wild geese	111
Thank you so much for your questions	32

The boy was barely five years old.   49

The first thing that you'll notice if   16

The flower-fed buffaloes of the spring   129

The sounds in the evening   127

The Vulture eats between his meals,   148

The whisky on your breath   89

The wombat lives across the seas,   106

There are many who say that a dog has its day,   69

There are strange things done in the midnight sun   132

There was no magic spell: 19

There's a whisper down the line at 11.39   117

'There's something new in the river,'   14

These I have loved . . .   120

They call to one another   71

They hunt, the velvet tigers in the jungle,   116

This is the Night Mail crossing the Border,   92

Today is very boring,   22

'Twas the voice of the sweet dove   104

'Under the ground   87

Waiter, there's a sky in my pie   30

We love to squeeze bananas,   15

We who play under the pines,   113

What is the opposite of *riot*?   53

When Aunty Jane   77

When fishes flew and forests walked,   141

When green buds hang in the elm like dust   158

When I was three I had a friend   6

When Noah left the Ark, the animals   57

Whenever I walk in a London Street,   124

When you wake up at night   9

Who saw the petals   84

Who's killed the leaves?   42

Whose woods these are I think I know.   139

Within the flower there lies a seed,   90

Yesterday I bought a penny fiddle   110

BIOGRAPHICAL NOTES

JOHN AGARD was born in 1949 in Guyana. He has lived in England since 1977. A popular performer of poetry for children and adults, his publications include *Limbo Dancer in Dark Glasses* (1983) and, for children, *Say It Again, Granny!* (1986), *Laughter is an Egg* (1990), *Get Back, Pimple* (1996) and *We Animals Would Like a Word with You* (1996).

ALLAN AHLBERG was born in 1938 in London. He writes poetry and fiction for children, and many of his books are illustrated by his late wife, Janet Ahlberg. His collections of poems include *Please Mrs Butler* (1983) and *Heard it in the Playground* (1989).

W. H. (WYSTAN HUGH) AUDEN (1907–73) was born in York. He was the pre-eminent British poet of the 1930s. He emigrated to New York in 1939 and became an American citizen in 1946. Major publications include *Poems* (1930) and *The Shield of Achilles* (1955). His *Collected Shorter Poems: 1927–1957* appeared in 1966.

GEORGE BARKER (1913–1991) was born in Essex but grew up in a tenement in Chelsea. He was associated with Dylan Thomas and the neo-Romantic movement of the 1940s. Among his many books of poetry since then are *Collected Poems* (1987) and three collections for children, including *To Aylsham Fair* (1970).

HILAIRE BELLOC (1870–1953) was born in France of Anglo-French parentage. He was brought up in England. An eminent novelist and man of letters in his day, he is remembered chiefly for his books of children's verse. These include *The Bad Child's Book of Beasts* (1896) and *Cautionary Tales for Children* (1907).

JAMES BERRY was born in 1924 in Jamaica. Since 1948 he has lived in England. He was editor of the anthology of Afro-Caribbean poetry *News for Babylon* (1984). His own poetry collections include *Lucy's Letters and Loving* (1982). For children, he has written the picture book *Celebration Song* (1994) and poetry collections including *When I Dance* (1988) and *Playing a Dazzler* (1996). He was awarded an OBE in 1990.

SIR JOHN BETJEMAN (1906–84) was born in London. He became a school-teacher and later wrote books on architecture and the English landscape. His poems reflect similar interests. In 1972 he was appointed Poet Laureate. His publications include *Collected Poems* (1962) and his verse-autobiography *Summoned by Bells* (1960).

N. M. (NIELS MOGENS) BODECKER was born in 1922 in Copenhagen. He published poems in Danish before emigrating to the United States in 1952. He illustrated children's books and later began to write for children. Publications include *Let's Marry Said the Cherry and Other Nonsense Poems* (1974) and *Snowman Sniffles and Other Verse* (1983).

RUPERT BROOKE (1887–1915) was born in Rugby. He was prominent among the Georgian poets before the outbreak of the First World War. He served on the Western Front and later died of blood-poisoning near the Greek island of Scyros, where he is buried. *Collected Poems* appeared in 1918.

CHARLES CAUSLEY was born in 1917 in Cornwall, where he continues to live. He retired from teaching in 1976 to become a full-time writer. Among his collections of poetry for children are *Figure of 8* (1969), *Figgie Hobbin* (1970), *Early in the Morning: A Collection of New Poems* (1986) and *Going to the Fair: Selected Poems for Children* (1994). He was awarded a CBE in 1986.

G. K. (GILBERT KING) CHESTERTON (1874–1936) was born in London. He was a prolific man of letters and a Catholic apologist. He also created the popular detective Father Brown, who first appeared in *The Innocence of Father Brown* (1911). His poetry publications include *The Wild Knight* (1900) and *Poems* (1915).

LEONARD CLARK (1905–81) was born in Guernsey. He worked as an Inspector of Schools until retirement in 1970. He wrote poetry for adults and children. Among his children's books are *Collected Poems and Verses for Children* (1975) and *The Singing Time* (1980).

ELIZABETH COATSWORTH (1893–1986) was born in Buffalo, New York. She wrote numerous stories for children and also published verse and fiction for adults. Among her poetry collections for children are *Night and the Cat* (1950) and *The Peaceable Kingdom and Other Poems* (1958).

E. E. (EDWARD ESTLIN) CUMMINGS (1894–1962) was born in Cambridge, Massachusetts. He served in the Ambulance Corps during the First World War and was interned in France. His poetry, which makes inventive use of typography, is collected in *Complete Poems* (1968). *Hist Whist* (1983) is a selection he made for children.

ROALD DAHL (1916–90) was born in Glamorgan, Wales, of Norwegian parents. His first children's story, *The Gremlins* (1943), was illustrated by the Walt Disney Studio. *The BFG* (1982) and *Revolting Rhymes* (1982) are among his many highly successful books for children. *Matilda* (1988) became a major feature film of the same name. Of his adult fiction, *Tales of the Unexpected* (1979) became a television series.

W. H. (WILLIAM HENRY) DAVIES (1871–1940) was born in Newport, Wales. His *Autobiography of a Super-Tramp* (1908) recounts his adventurous life until a train accident in Canada caused him to lose a leg. Thereafter he settled down to write the poetry collected in *The Complete Poems of W. H. Davies* (1963).

WALTER DE LA MARE (1873–1956) was born in Kent. He worked as a book-keeper until 1908, when he was granted a Civil List pension. *The Listeners and Other Poems* (1912) brought him enduring fame. Later publications include the anthology for young readers *Come Hither* (1923) and *Poems for Children* (1930).

MICHAEL DUGAN was born in 1947 in Melbourne, Australia. He has edited various publications, including the children's magazine *Puffinalia*. Among his books of poems for adults are *Missing People* (1970) and, for children, *Stuff and Nonsense* (1974) and *Nonsense Places* (1976).

RICHARD EDWARDS was born in 1949 in Kent. He has lived in Italy and France and is a part-time teacher. His books of children's verse include *The Word Party* (1986), *A Mouse in my Roof* (1988), *If Only* (1990), *The House that Caught a Cold* (1991) and *Leopards on Mars* (1993).

T. S. (THOMAS STEARNS) ELIOT (1888–1965) was born in St Louis, Missouri. From 1914 he lived in England and, in 1925, he became a director of Faber. He received the Nobel Prize for Literature in 1948. His publications include *The Waste Land* (1922), *Murder in the Cathedral* (1935) and a book of light verse, *Old Possum's Book of Practical Cats* (1939).

ELEANOR FARJEON (1881–1965) was born in London. She wrote stories and poems for children and published more than eighty books. Among the best known are *Kings and Queens* (1932), written in collaboration with her brother Herbert, and *The Little Bookroom* (1955).

MAX FATCHEN was born in 1920 near Adelaide, Australia. He has written several stories for young readers inspired by the sea and by his travels in the outback and along Australia's rivers. His poetry for children includes *Songs for My Dog and Other People* (1980) and *Wry Rhymes for Troublesome Times* (1983).

RACHEL FIELD (1894–1942) was born in New York City. One of her novels for adults, *All This and Heaven Too* (1938), became a successful film. But she is best remembered for her children's story *Hitty, Her First Hundred Years* (1929) and for her collection of children's verse *Taxis and Toadstools* (1926).

ROBERT FROST (1874–1963) was born in San Francisco. He spent most of his life in New England and his poetry, collected in *The Poetry of Robert Frost* (1969), is closely associated with its landscape. In later life he was a friend of President Kennedy and read a poem at his Inauguration.

MARY GILMORE (1865–1962) was born in New South Wales, Australia. She was a teacher, a journalist and a crusading trade-unionist. She published several collections of poems for adults, including *The Passionate Heart* (1918) and *Fourteen Men* (1954).

HARRY GRAHAM (1874–1936) was born in London. He was a captain in the Coldstream Guards. He wrote light verse for adults. Poems from two of his books, *Ruthless Rhymes for Heartless Homes* (1899) and *More Ruthless Rhymes for Heartless Homes* (1930), have become favourites with children.

ROBERT GRAVES (1895–1985) was born in London. From 1929 he made Majorca his home. He published many collections of poems and was a prolific writer of books on classical subjects, including the novel *I, Claudius* (1934). His poetry for children includes *The Penny Fiddle* (1960) and *Ann of Highwood Hall* (1964).

THOMAS HARDY (1840–1928) spent most of his life in his native Dorset. Between 1871 and 1895 he published his novels of country life. Both *Tess of the d'Urbervilles* (1891) and *Jude the Obscure* (1895) provoked controversy, and thereafter he concentrated on poetry. *Wessex Poems* (1898) was followed by eight more collections.

JOHN HEATH–STUBBS was born in 1918 in London. He was an English lecturer until 1973 and has taught at universities in Egypt and America. He became blind in the 1970s and now composes his poems in his head. Publications include *Collected Poems: 1943–1987* (1988) and, for young readers, *A Parliament of Birds* (1975).

ADRIAN HENRI was born in 1932 in Birkenhead. He is associated with the Liverpool Poets and was included in *The Mersey Sound: Penguin Modern Poets 10* (1967). He is also a painter. Publications for children include *The Phantom Lollipop Lady* (1986), *The Rhinestone Rhino and Other Poems* (1989), *Robocat* (1998) and *The World's Your Lobster* (1998).

MARY ANN HOBERMAN was born in 1930 in Connecticut. She writes stories and poems for children, and many of her books are illustrated by her husband, Norman Hoberman. Among her poetry publications are *All My Shoes Come in Two's* (1957), *Not Enough Beds for the Babies* (1965) and *Fathers, Mothers, Sisters, Brothers* (1991).

A. E. (ALFRED EDWARD) HOUSMAN (1859–1936) was born in Worcestershire, although it is neighbouring Shropshire that features in his poems. He was a notable classical scholar and in 1911 became Professor of Latin at Cambridge. *A Shropshire Lad* (1896) was followed by *Last Poems* (1922) and *More Poems* (1936).

LIBBY HOUSTON was born in 1941 in London. She has contributed poetry programmes to the BBC Schools series *Pictures in Your Mind* and has published one collection of children's poetry, *All Change*. Her adult collections include *Plain Clothes* (1971) and *At the Mercy* (1981).

TED HUGHES (1930–1998) was born in Yorkshire. He was married to Sylvia Plath until her death in 1963. His poetry for children includes *Season Songs* (1975) and *Moon-Bells and Other Poems* (1978), and he edited, with Seamus Heaney, *The Rattle Bag* (1982). He became Poet Laureate in 1984. Adult titles include *Tales from Ovid: Twenty-Four Passages from the 'Metamorphoses'* and *The Birthday Letters* both published in 1998.

ELIZABETH JENNINGS was born in 1926 in Lincolnshire. She worked at Oxford City Library and then as a publisher's reader. Since 1961 she has been a freelance writer. Her poetry publications include *Collected Poems: 1953–1985* (1986) and, for children, *The Secret Brother* (1969), *After the Ark* (1978) and *A Spell of Words* (1997).

RUDYARD KIPLING (1865–1936) was born in Bombay of English parents. From 1899 he lived most of his life in England as a full-time writer. He received the Nobel Prize for Literature in 1907. His classic books for children are *The Jungle Book* (1894), *Kim* (1901) and the *Just So Stories* (1902).

PHILIP LARKIN (1922–85) was born in Coventry. From 1955 he was Librarian at the University of Hull. He was associated with the Movement poets of the 1950s and published three acclaimed volumes of poems, *The Less Deceived* (1955), *The Whitsun Weddings* (1964) and *High Windows* (1974). *Collected Poems* appeared in 1988.

DENNIS LEE was born in 1939 in Toronto. He is a poet, editor and critic. He also writes for children and, from 1982 to 1986, was a songwriter for the television programme *Fraggle Rock*. His collections of children's poetry include *Alligator Pie* (1974) and *Jelly Belly* (1983). *Nightwatch* (1996) is one of his recent adult collections.

LAURIE LEE (1914–1997) was born in Gloucestershire. He was well known for his books of autobiography, *Cider with Rosie* (1959) and *As I Walked Out One Midsummer Morning* (1969). Three early volumes of poetry are reprinted in *Selected Poems* (1983).

VACHEL LINDSAY (1879–1931) was born in Illinois. He was a minstrel-poet who in his youth exchanged his poems for food and lodgings. A popular performer, he none the less died, poor and in ill health, by suicide. Publications include *The Tramp's Excuse and Other Poems* (1909) and *Going-to-the-Stars* (1926).

EDWARD LOWBURY was born in 1913 in London. He is a doctor and worked in the field of medical research until his retirement. His collections of poems include *Time For Sale* (1961), *Apollo* (1990), *Mystic Bridge* (1997) and, for children, *Green Magic* (1972).

NORMAN MACCAIG (1910–1996) was born in Edinburgh. He worked as a teacher until 1970 and then held positions at the universities of Edinburgh and Stirling. His books of poems include *Riding Lights* (1955) and *Rings on a Tree* (1968). His *Collected Poems* appeared in 1985.

ROGER MCGOUGH was born in 1937 in Liverpool. He is one of the Liverpool Poets who appeared in *The Mersey Sound: Penguin Modern Poets 10* (1967). His poems often appeal equally to adults and to children. Publications include *In the Glassroom* (1976), *Selected Poems* (1989) and, specifically for children, *Sky in the Pie* (1983), *Pillow Talk* (1990) and *Bad Bad Cats* (1997). He was awarded an OBE in 1977.

JOHN MASEFIELD (1878–1967) was born in Herefordshire. He was a sailor in his youth, and the sea features in the many ballads and narrative poems that he wrote. In 1930 he was appointed Poet Laureate. His books of poems include *Salt-Water Ballads* (1902) and *Reynard the Fox* (1919).

EVE MERRIAM was born in 1916 in New York City. She has worked on radio, as a teacher and in publishing. She writes for both adults and children. Among her poetry collections for the young are *There Is No Rhyme for Silver* (1962), *It Doesn't Always Have to Rhyme* (1964), *Higgle·Wiggle: Happy Rhymes* (1994) and *You Be Good & I'll Be Night: Jump-On-The-Bed Poems* (1996).

SPIKE MILLIGAN was born in 1918 in India. He was a star of the *Goon Show*, a radio comedy famous from the 1950s, and is well known as a television personality. His humorous books for children include *Silly Verse for Kids* (1959), *Unspun Socks from a Chicken's Laundry* (1981) and *Startling Verse for All the Family* (1987). He was awarded an honorary CBE in 1992.

A. A. (ALAN ALEXANDER) MILNE (1882–1956) was born in London. He was a successful dramatist. But it is the books written for his son, Christopher Robin, that have become classics: *Winnie-the-Pooh* (1926), *The House at Pooh Corner* (1928) and, in verse, *When We Were Very Young* (1924) and *Now We Are Six* (1927).

ADRIAN MITCHELL was born in 1932 in London. He writes in various media for adults and children. *Love Songs of World War III* (1989) is a collection of lyrics from his plays and shows. Poetry publications include *For Beauty Douglas: Collected Poems 1953–1979* (1982) and, for children, *Nothingmas Day* (1984) and *Balloon Lagoon and the Magic Islands of Poetry* (1997).

EDWIN MORGAN was born in 1920 in Glasgow. From 1947 he taught at Glasgow University and was Professor of English there from 1975 to 1985. He has translated several Eastern European poets. Collections of his own poetry include *Selected Poems* (1985), *Themes on a Variation* (1988) and *Virtual and Other Realities* (1997).

OGDEN NASH (1902–71) was born in New York State. He began as a serious poet but then turned, with spectacular success, to light verse. He published several books specifically for children, but adults and young readers alike enjoy the poems in such collections as *The Primrose Path* (1955).

GRACE NICHOLS was born in 1950 in Guyana. She worked there as a journalist and reporter, before coming to Britain in 1977 and has since published several books of poems for adults including *The Fat Black Woman's Poems* (1984), *Lazy Thoughts of a Lazy Woman* (1989) and *Sunris* (1996). Her children's poetry collections include *Give Yourself A Hug* (1994) and *No Hickory, No Dickory, No Dock* with John Agard (1996).

GARETH OWEN was born in 1936 in Lancashire. He has worked in theatre in Birmingham as an actor and director. His collections of poems for children include *Song of the City* (1985), *Salford Road and Other Poems* (1988), *My Granny is a Sumo Wrestler* (1994) and *The Fox on the Roundabout* (1995).

WILFRED OWEN (1893–1918) was born in Shropshire. He is regarded as the foremost poet of the First World War, during which he wrote his mature poetry. He was killed a week before the Armistice. *Poems* (1920) was edited by Siegfried Sassoon. *Collected Poems* appeared in 1963.

A. B. (ANDREW BARTON) 'BANJO' PATERSON (1864–1941) was born in New South Wales, Australia. Although a qualified solicitor, he lived an adventurous life as war correspondent, newspaper editor and grazier. He published several books of popular ballads, including *The Man from Snowy River* (1895), and one book for children, *The Animals Noah Forgot* (1933).

BRIAN PATTEN was born in Liverpool in 1946. His poetry for adults has been published in many languages and his collections include *Love Poems* (1981), *Storm Damage* (1988), *Grinning Jack* (1990) and *Armada* (1996). His work for children includes the poetry collections *Gargling with Jelly* (1985), *Thawing Frozen Frogs* (1990), *The Utter Nutters* (1994) and *Mouse Poems* (1998), as well as plays, the award-winning novel *Mr Moon's Last Case* and the picture book *Emma's Doll* (1998).

MERVYN PEAKE (1911–68) was born in China. He was a gifted artist and illustrator of children's books. His poetry for children includes *Rhymes Without Reason* (1944) and *A Book of Nonsense* (1972). His best-known work of fiction for adults is his 'Titus' trilogy, beginning with *Titus Groan* (1946).

LYDIA PENDER was born in 1907 in London. She has lived most of her life in Australia. She writes stories and poems for children. Among her publications are *Barnaby and the Horses* (1961) and her collected poems for children, *Morning Magpie* (1984).

JACK PRELUTSKY was born in 1940 in New York City. He is author of more than thirty collections of children's poetry, including *The Queen of Eene* (1970), *Nightmares* (1976), *The New Kid on the Block* (1984), *The Dragons are Singing Tonight* (1993) and *A Pizza the Size of the Sun* (1996).

KATHARINE PYLE (1863–1938) was born in Delaware, where she lived in the family house at Wilmington until her death. Many of her poems were illustrated by her brother, Howard Pyle, himself a well-known children's writer. Publications include *Careless Jane and Other Tales* (1904) and *The Pearl Fairy Book* (1923).

KATHLEEN RAINE was born in 1908 in London. She is the author of several books on William Blake and other romantic poets. Her own poetry publications include *The Year One* (1932), *Collected Poems: 1935–1980* (1981) and *Living With Mystery* (1992).

JAMES REEVES (1909–78) was born in London. He edited and wrote many books on poets and poetry. He also wrote poems for adults but is best known for his children's verse. His publications include *How to Write Poems for Children* (1971) and *Complete Poems for Children* (1973).

E. V. (EMILE VICTOR) RIEU (1887–1972) was born in London. He was editor of Penguin Classics from 1944 to 1964 and himself translated *The Odyssey* (1946). He published two books of children's verse, *Cuckoo Calling: A Book of Verse for Youthful People* (1933) and *The Flattered Flying Fish and Other Poems* (1962).

THEODORE ROETHKE (1908–63) was born in Michigan. From 1947 he taught at the University of Washington. His poems reflect his childhood intimacy with his father's greenhouses, notably in *The Lost Son* (1948). Other publications include his collected poems for children, *I Am! Says the Lamb* (1961).

MICHAEL ROSEN was born in 1946 in Harrow, Middlesex. He writes stories and poems for children. He is a popular performer of his work and a well-known advocate of children's books. He won the Eleanor Farjeon Award in 1997 for his contribution to children's literature. Poetry collections include *Mind Your Own Business* (1974), *Wouldn't You Like To Know* (1977), *Quick, Let's Get Out of Here* (1983) and *You Wait Till I'm Older Than You!* (1996).

A. L. (ALFRED LESLIE) ROWSE (1903–1997) was born in Cornwall, the setting for many of his poems and autobiographical books. He was an eminent historian and was a Fellow of All Souls College, Oxford, from 1925 to 1974. His *Collected Poems* appeared in 1981.

VERNON SCANNELL was born in 1922 in Lincolnshire. He was a boxer before becoming a teacher of English. Since 1962 he has been a full-time writer. His publications include *New and Collected Poems: 1950–1980* (1980) and, for children, *The Apple Raid and Other Poems* (1974) and *The Clever Potato* (1988). More poems for children appear in the anthology *We Couldn't Provide Fish Thumbs* (1997).

IAN SERRAILLIER (1912–1994) was born in London. He was a schoolmaster until 1961, after which he devoted his time to his children's writing. Publications include the poetry collection *Thomas and the Sparrow* (1946) and the novel *The Silver Sword* (1956), which has been serialized for television.

ROBERT SERVICE (1874–1958) was born in Preston and lived in Glasgow until he was twenty-one. He emigrated to western Canada and there began to write his popular ballads. These include *Songs of a Sourdough* (1907) and *Ballads of a Cheechako* (1909).

SHEL SILVERSTEIN was born in 1932 in Chicago. He is a cartoonist, composer and folk-singer as well as a children's poet. Among his publications are *Where the Sidewalk Ends* (1974), *A Light in the Attic* (1981) and *Falling Up: Poems and Drawings* (1996).

STEVIE SMITH (1902–71) was born in Hull. When she was three she moved to London with her family and lived in the same house until her death. Her poetry collections, each illustrated with her own drawings, include *Not Waving But Drowning* (1957) and *The Scorpion and Other Poems* (1972).

DYLAN THOMAS (1914–53) was born in Swansea. He was the leading poet among the neo-Romantics of the 1940s. His early death, during a reading tour in America, was due largely to alcoholism. Publications include *Collected Poems* (1952) and a play for television and radio, *Under Milk Wood* (1954).

EDWARD THOMAS (1878–1917) was born in London. He was a freelance writer until, at the age of thirty-six, he met Robert Frost. He began to write poems and composed steadily until his death, three years later, in France at the Battle of Arras. *Collected Poems* appeared in 1920.

W. J. (WALTER JAMES) TURNER (1889–1946) was born in Melbourne, Australia. He moved to London when he was seventeen and worked as a music and drama critic. He wrote novels and published several collections of poetry, including *The Hunter and Other Poems* (1916) and *The Dark Fire* (1918).

JOHN WALSH (1911–72) was born in Brighton. He was an English teacher and wrote poems for children. His published work includes *The Roundabout by the Sea* (1960) and *The Truants and Other Poems for Children* (1965).

RICHARD WILBUR was born in 1921 in New York City. He has taught at Harvard and other universities in America, and in 1987 he became the American Poet Laureate. His publications include *New and Selected Poems* (1988) and, for children, *Loudmouse* (1963), *Opposites* (1973) and *The Disappearing Alphabet* (1998).

NANCY WILLARD was born in 1936 in Ann Arbor, Michigan. She writes for both children and adults. Among her publications for children are the storybook *Simple Pictures Are Best* (1977) and the poetry collections *A Visit to William Blake's Inn* (1981) and *An Alphabet of Angels* (1994).

MARGARET WISE BROWN (1910–52) was born in New York City. She was a prolific writer of stories for children, including several under the pseudonym Golden MacDonald. Her poetry for children includes *The Dark Wood of the Golden Birds* (1950) and *Nibble Nibble* (1959).

JUDITH WRIGHT was born in 1915 in New South Wales, Australia. *The Moving Image: Poems* (1946) established her as an important Australian poet. She has published many collections since and has edited *A Book of Australian Verse* (1968). She has also written stories for children, including *King of the Dingoes* (1959). Her *Collected Poems* appeared in 1994.

KIT WRIGHT was born in 1944 in Kent. He taught at Brock University, Canada, for three years and has been a Fellow Commoner at Cambridge. His publications include *Poems 1974–1983* (1988) and, for children, *Hot Dog and Other Poems* (1981), *Cat Among the Pigeons* (1987) and *Great Snakes!* (1994).

W. B. (WILLIAM BUTLER) YEATS (1865–1939) was born in Dublin. He was the leading figure of the Irish literary revival and a founder of the Abbey Theatre. He served for six years in the Irish Senate. In 1923 he received the Nobel Prize for Literature. *Collected Poems* appeared in 1950.

BENJAMIN ZEPHANIAH was born in 1958 in Birmingham. He spent some of his early years in Jamaica which has had a dramatic effect on his work. He is well-known for his 'rap' style making his poetry highly accessible and very modern. His publications include *City Psalms* (1992) and *Propa Propaganda* (1996) and, for children, *Talking Turkeys* (1994) and *Funky Chickens* (1996).

ACKNOWLEDGEMENTS

The publishers gratefully acknowledge the following for permission to reproduce copyright material in this book.

By kind permission of John Agard c/o Caroline Sheldon Literary Agency 'Don't Call Alligator Long-Mouth Till You Cross River' from *Say It Again, Granny!* published by Bodley Head 1986 and 'Hatch Me A Riddle' from *Laughter is an Egg* published by Penguin Books 1990; 'Billy McBone' by Allan Ahlberg from *Heard It in the Playground*, first published by Viking 1989, copyright ©Allan Ahlberg, 1989, and 'I did a bad thing once' by Allan Ahlberg from *Please Mrs Butler* first published by Kestrel 1983, copyright © Allan Ahlberg, 1983, both by permission of Penguin Books Ltd; 'Night Mail' by W. H. Auden from *Collected Poems* reprinted by permission of Faber and Faber Ltd; 'They Call to One Another' by George Barker from *To Aylsham Fair* reprinted by permission of Faber and Faber Ltd; 'The Frog' and 'The Vulture' by Hilaire Belloc from *The Complete Verse of Hilaire Belloc*, copyright © Hilaire Belloc, reprinted by permission of The Peters Fraser and Dunlop Group Limited on behalf of the Estate of Hilaire Belloc; 'Dreaming Black Boy' by James Berry from *When I Dance*, copyright © James Berry, reprinted by permission of The Peters Fraser and Dunlop Group Limited; 'Diary of a Church Mouse' by John Betjeman from *Collected Poems* reprinted by permission of John Murray (Publishers); 'Perfect Arthur' by N. M. Bodecker from *Let's Marry Said the Cherry* reprinted by permission of Faber and Faber Ltd; 'Tom Bone' and 'Colonel Fazackerley' by Charles Causley from *Collected Poems* published by Macmillan 1975, reprinted by permission of David Higham Associates; 'The Donkey' by G. K. Chesterton, reprinted by permission of A. P. Watt Ltd on behalf of The Royal Literary Fund; 'Good Company' by Leonard Clark from *Good Company* published by Dobson Books Ltd, copyright © Leonard Clark, reprinted by permission of The Literary Executor of Leonard Clark; 'maggie and milly and molly and may' by E. E. Cummings from *Complete Poems 1904–1962*, edited by George J. Firmage, reprinted by permission of W. W. Norton & Company, copyright © 1991 by the Trustees for the E. E. Cummings Trust and George James Firmage; 'Down With Children! Do Them In!' by Roald Dahl from *The Witches* published by Jonathan Cape and Penguin Books Ltd, reprinted by permission of David Higham Associates; 'The Blind Boxer' and 'The Happy Child' by W. H. Davies, reprinted by permission of Dee & Griffin acting for the Trustee of the Estate of W. H. Davies; 'Tom's Angel', 'The Scarecrow' and 'A Robin' by Walter de la Mare from *Collected Poems*, reprinted by permission of The Literary Trustees of Walter de la Mare, and the Society of Authors as their representative; 'Nightening' by Michael Dugan from *Flocks, Socks and Other Shocks* published by Penguin Books Australia Ltd, reprinted by kind permission of the author; 'When I Was Three' and 'The Word Party' by Richard Edwards from *The Word Party* published by Lutterworth Press 1986, copyright © Richard Edwards, 1986, by permission of Lutterworth Press; 'Skimbleshanks' by T. S. Eliot from *Old Possum's Book of Practical Cats*, published by Faber and Faber Ltd 1939, reprinted by permission of Faber and Faber Ltd; 'The Distance' by Eleanor Farjeon from *Silver-Sand and Snow*, published by Michael Joseph 1951, copyright © Gervase Farjeon, and 'The Sounds in the Evening' by Eleanor Farjeon from *Invitation to a Mouse* published by Hodder and Stoughton both by permission of David Higham Associates; an extract from 'Ruinous Rhymes' by Max Fatchen from *Wry Rhymes for Troublesome Times* published by Kestrel Books 1983, copyright © Max Fatchen, 1983, reprinted by permission of Penguin Books Ltd; 'Something Told the Wild Geese' by Rachel Field from *Poems* published by Macmillan 1934, copyright © Macmillan Publishing Company, 1934, copyright © renewed by Arthur S. Pederson, 1962, reprinted by permission of Simon & Schuster Books for Young Readers, an imprint of Simon & Schuster Children's Publishing Division; 'Stopping by Woods on a Snowy Evening' and 'A Minor Bird' by Robert Frost from *The Poetry of Robert Frost*, published by Jonathan Cape, edited by Edward Connery Latham, copyright 1951, © 1956 by Robert Frost, copyright 1923, copyright 1928, copyright © 1969 by Henry Holt and Company, Inc., reprinted by permission of Jonathan Cape, The Estate of Robert Frost and Henry Holt and Company, Inc.; 'The Wild Horses' by Mary Gilmore from *Selected Poems* reprinted by permission of ETT Imprint, Sydney 1998; 'The Alice Jean' and 'The Penny Fiddle' by Robert Graves from *Complete Poems* reprinted by permission of Carcanet Press Limited; 'The Kingfisher' by John Heath-Stubbs from *A Charm Against Toothache* reprinted by permission of David Higham Associates; 'Best Friends' by Adrian Henri from *The Phantom Lollipop Lady and Other Poems*, published by Methuen Books 1986, copyright © Adrian Henri, 1986, reprinted by permission of Rogers, Coleridge & White Ltd; 'When Green Buds Hang' by A. E. Housman reprinted by permission of The Society of Authors as the Literary Representative of the Estate of A. E. Housman; 'The Dream of the Cabbage Caterpillars' and 'The Old Woman and the Sandwiches' by Libby Houston from *All Change*, published by Oxford University Press 1993, copyright © Libby Houston, 1993, by kind permission of the author; 'Leaves' by Ted Hughes from *Season Songs* reprinted by permission of Faber